Going to Court in TEXAS

Riding the Circuit

1842-1861

Richard B. Marrin
and
Lorna Geer Sheppard

HERITAGE BOOKS
2007

HERITAGE BOOKS
AN IMPRINT OF HERITAGE BOOKS, INC.

Books, CDs, and more—Worldwide

For our listing of thousands of titles see our website
at
www.HeritageBooks.com

Published 2007 by
HERITAGE BOOKS, INC.
Publishing Division
65 East Main Street
Westminster, Maryland 21157-5026

Other books by the authors:

Abstracts from The Northern Standard *and* The Red River District *[Texas]: August 20, 1842-August 19, 1848*

Other books by Richard B. Marrin:

A Glance Back in Time: Life in Colonial New Jersey (1704-1770) As Depicted in News Accounts of the Day

The Paradise of Texas, Volume 1: Clarksville and Red River County, 1846-1860

Passage Point: An Amateur's Dig Into New Jersey's Colonial Past

Runaways of Colonial New Jersey: Indentured Servants, Slaves, Deserters, and Prisoners, 1720-1781

International Standard Book Number: 978-0-7884-4299-

In Memory of our friend and mentor,
Arthur Mitchell

Table of Contents

Chapter One

Through Whose Eyes

Charles DeMorse led an interesting life.

He had come to Texas in 1836, a young lawyer from New York's even then fabled Wall Street, part of a brigade of volunteers from that city, intent on helping Texas win her independence from Mexico. He served first as a lieutenant of Marines in the Texas Navy and, later, as a major in the Army. After Independence, DeMorse resumed the practice of law, not in New York but in Matagorda, Texas, a settlement of 1,650 transplanted New Englanders at the mouth of the Colorado River as it emptied into the Gulf of Mexico. He also began dabbling in newspapers, becoming a journalist for the *Daily Bulletin* in Austin, reporting on the activities of the Texas legislature.

Convinced by the leading citizens of the Red River District of the need for a newspaper for their vast region and its increasing population, DeMorse in 1842 founded, edited, published, and owned *The Northern Standard*, a weekly newspaper. Over the next forty six years, the paper would grow to become the second largest in circulation in Texas and DeMorse himself would be hailed as *the Father of Texas Journalism*. The *Standard,* to which the paper's name would be officially shortened, considered itself a voice of the "Democratic" party, at least after Texas completed its annexation to the United States in 1846 and became a two party system. DeMorse's influence on behalf of the Democrats earned him another title: *The Father of the Democratic Press in Texas*. During the Civil War, DeMorse would serve as colonel in the Confederate Calvary. He would even be nominated twice for Governor of the State in 1873 and 1886.[1]

Despite these other interests, DeMorse remained a practicing lawyer from 1842 until he went off to war in 1862, two decades later.

In Texas then, judges, the prosecuting attorney and the

rest of the trial bar would twice annually ride the "circuit", going from county to county within their District, and spending a week or more in each county seat trying cases. DeMorse welcomed the chance to visit all of North Texas, as far south as Dallas and Fort Worth. It let him solicit new subscribers and advertisers for *The Standard* and dun the tardy payers, of whom there seemed to be many. He also reported back to his readers as to conditions in these new frontier settlements, fascinating dispatches, that, accumulated over years and years of his court visits, accurately chronicle the growth of these towns from the time they were stakes in the ground.

Historians are blessed by this treasure trove of details about daily life in Texas, while it was a Republic and in its early years of statehood. The Texas legal profession is equally blessed by it. In his reports home to the readers about his travels on horse back across Northern Texas, DeMorse has preserved an image of what it meant to practice law - *"Going to Court in Texas*" is how he put it - more than a century and a half ago.

Next time today's lawyer sits at Hobby Airport awaiting a delayed flight to another city for a court appearance next morning; the next time today's lawyer is stuck in a traffic jam on Highway 35 south, trying to get downtown Dallas to court; the next time today's lawyer laments being unable to bill his time driving the sixty miles from county seat to county seat to attend court, then let those lawyers consider the dangerous swollen rivers that had to be crossed on horseback, the times it took two days to travel but thirty miles in mud and driven rain, and, sleeping in wet blankets in the rain, on the nights too dark and the road too unknown to venture farther.

However, if today's attorneys enjoy the excitement of practicing law, the camaraderie that exists within the profession and among its members and the good times that happen among the like minded, then let them consider the dances, horse races, speeches and entertainment that accompanied "Court Week" back then - a week or more of commercial and social frenzy whose start the arrival of the visiting lawyers signaled. Consider also the exciting discoveries, natural and historical, the band of lawyers encountered in their travels by horseback across a land that was still new and could surprise the rider.

Chapter Two

The Texas Court System before the Civil War

The Texas Court system is *sui generis*, both in its origin and practice.

Courts existed in Texas as far back as Stephen Austin's colony. In 1822, he appointed Josiah H. Bell as provisional Justice of the Peace for the province of Mexican Texas. The Mexican authorities, however, disapproved. Three *alcaldes* were appointed instead, who were part judges, part administrators and had both civil and criminal jurisdiction.

The Anglo colonists, more familiar with the English common law of the Anglo Saxon, not the Roman tradition,[2] disliked a system that deprived them, among other things, of the right to a jury trial and the writ of *habeas corpus*.

The Texas Revolution in 1835 permitted Texans to remake the court system and they adopted essentially an Anglo-American scheme of courts. The Constitution provided for a Supreme Court to hear only appeals and a set of inferior Courts as the Congress of the Republic would design. Congress was also empowered by the Texas Constitution to divide the Republic into Judicial Districts[3], each to have a trial judge.[4] All Supreme Court and District Court Judges were elected by Congress.

Upon annexation to the United states as its 28th state, the new Constitution carried over the court system of the Republic without modification. In 1850, the Constitution was amended to make the Judges elective, a practice that has continued ever since, except during the dark days of Reconstruction.[5]

The District Courts, then as now, were trial courts of general jurisdiction in law and in equity.[6] They handled criminal felonies, divorces , election contests, liens on real estate and civil actions of every variety. Each county had its branch of the multi county District Court.[7] Each county also had its own county courts[8] and Justices of the Peace, who were elected by the people.

DeMorse and his band of traveling lawyers focused on Northern Texas, along the Red River as far west as Palo Pinto. They rode to Johnson, Ellis and Navarro counties, south of Dallas and Fort Worth. Most of his activity was in the 8th Judicial District, which for some of the 1850s was comprised of the counties of Bowie, Cass, Marion, Titus[9], Hunt[10], Hopkins, Fannin, Lamar and Red River.[11] DeMorse and his fellow riders appeared fairly regularly to Collin, Dallas, Kaufman, Cooke, Grayson, Denton, Tarrant and Wise counties, some of which were in the 9th Judicial District. As the frontier went westward, so did the stalwart band of counsel, often inaugurating court in counties like Parker, Montague, Johnson, Ellis and Upshur.

The Standard of March 29, 1856 published the Court schedule for the Spring term of that year:

> *Collin & Titus, both two weeks begin on April 12th*
> *Grayson (two weeks) begins April 12th*
> *Hopkins (one week) begin April 26th*
> *Hunt (one week) begins May 3*
> *Cooke is one week and Fannin is two and both begin on May 10*
> *Denton one week begins on May 17th*
> *Lamar's two weeks and begins on the May 24th*
> *Tarrant is two weeks and begins on June 24*
> *Dallas is July 1, until business is disposed of.*[12]

Of course, after Texas joined the United States, a Federal District Court was established to conduct trials in "diversity" cases, that is, one that has parties from two different states or a foreign national.[13] Unlike today, where there are four Federal Districts in Texas, in 1846 there was only one District. A circuit court, John C. Watrous was the first United States District Judge for Texas. It is now the Eastern District. As the population grew, a second Federal District Court was needed, so, in 1857, the Western District was formed and Thomas Howard Duval was appointed judge.[14]

Chapter Three

The First Court Houses

In those early days in Northern Texas, most of the population lived on farms in the countryside. The county court house became the center of law and authority in a region not far distant from the frontier. Often the court house was the first site laid out in a new county, its location being important for commercial reasons as well. The court house and the things that happened inside it, attracted people - out of town lawyers, plaintiffs, defendants, witnesses, jurors and the curious. Hotels, stores of different varieties and businesses, including the post office, hotels, doctors and lawyers offices, all hovered around the court house.

DeMorse tried cases in the court houses for all the counties of North Texas and was never shy in expressing an opinion about their comfort or utility. These comments provide us with a glimpse of what these first "Temples of Justices", as DeMorse called them, looked like.

Court houses came in a wide variety in those first days. In fact, some new counties had no courthouse at all! It was a detail that never seemed to bother DeMorse. He had, for example, some cases on the docket in Wise County the day it opened in 1856. "Court", he remarked "may be held under a tree as it has been before this, on our circuit."[15]

And well, it had been. In Mount Vernon, when it was county seat for Lamar County[16], court was held in Matt Click's tavern during the winter and under a large bois d'arc tree in the summer. In Denton county, when Pinckney was its county seat, court sat outside under a tree and the jury room, where deliberations were held, was a nearby thicket. When the county seat was moved to Sherman in 1848[17], Court was reportedly held for a while beneath a pecan tree. The tree reportedly doubled as a church on Sunday, a post office[18] and a bank.[19]

According to *The Texas Courthouse Revisited* , in the first years of Red River County (mother county to all or part of thirty nine present day North Texas counties) there was no courthouse. Other buildings were borrowed, when needed. For instance, Court was held on the second floor of different general stores, first at Travis Wright's store in Jonesboro, and then at Gunboat Latimer's in LaGrange (now Madras).

Holding court under a tree might seem a romantic notion but, as populations grew, litigating *au natural* was no longer alluring. Rather, nearby trees were chopped down and courthouses constructed from their logs[20], as were a great variety of other buildings in early Texas, including forts, blockhouses, chapels, jails, schools, stores, taverns, and inns.

Hunt County's first "Temple of Justice" at Greenville, for example, was built of logs in 1853. While some improvement over holding court outdoors in inclement weather, the new courthouse was not very comfortable either on rainy, cold and muddy days. One November day in 1857, DeMorse lamented: "The old shed of a court house is not fit to do any business in, except in pleasant weather, and unfortunately, there was little to do since the weather turned bad." [21]

Collin county's first courthouse, in its then county seat of Buckner, was also made of logs. Its replacement, when the court moved to McKinney, was equally unsatisfactory, according to DeMorse:

> *The old court house is one of the objectionable features. Originally, a poor building in bad taste and small, it is dilapidated, insufficient and gives a real bad representation to the real importance of the county, which exceeds in invariable fertility any other in the state and has a heavy, for Texas, population.*[22]

Bowie's first two courthouses were made of logs, the second one erected in 1848 being made out of sawed ones, an improvement of sorts. But, the latter was far from being comfortable when the weather was cold, which led to a scolding of the county. The outspoken DeMorse, with *The Standard,* had a pulpit from which to preach:

> *The excessive coldness of the weather*

prevented [the Judge's] appearance on Monday, but if he had been here, there was no provision for fire in the courtroom and business could not have been transacted without fire. On Wednesday morning, the Sheriff procured a stove and had the pipe run out a window. Bowie is quite able to put a chimney in its courthouse or otherwise provide for warmth and will find it economical to do this rather than to pay for jurors attendance, while it is so cold that they cannot sit in the courtroom.[23]

A similar complaint was lodged by DeMorse against Denton County and its primitive court house built in 1851 in its then county seat, Alton. DeMorse described it in 1856, just after the decision had been made to move the county seat to the town of Denton:

The District Court has been in session here, Judge Burford presiding, since Monday morning. Court is held in an open log house without fire and the sessions during the cold weather prevalent during the week might be considered uncomfortable, but here, where a part of the attendants on the court sit up around log hearths because [lodgings] cannot be got, no one grumbles much.[24]

Cooke County was another of DeMorse's least liked court houses. The county had had several court houses since it was formed in 1848. One story has it that the site of the county seat itself, Gainesville, was selected by Chief Justice Bob Wheelock, who, with a jug of whiskey in hand, called for "All in favor of putting the town here, come to me." The first courthouse was said to have cost $29. It was a 14 foot square log cabin, with a dirt floor and no chimney, which served also as the post office with the mail being handed out of the glass less window. According to legend, one time when the flies were so bad, a steer belonging to Jim Dixon went into the courthouse for shelter and, trying to get out, knocked the building down.[25] DeMorse confirms some of this: "Gainesville, the county seat of Cooke County, is made up of one residence, a small store and a log cabin, fourteen foot square, without a floor window or door, which is called the courthouse."[26]

The next year, DeMorse was not so charitable. He sarcastically described the sixteen foot square court house[27] in Gainesville, county seat of Cooke county, as "spacious and well ventilated", with good reason:

> *It has not yet a floor, a door or a window, but the light comes freely through between the logs, as the dust does when the wind is high." Inside, while the Court was in session, "the jury and the bar occupied rough puncheon benches, at the sides of the house and His Honor, by way of distinction, having a split bottomed chair, one of the four belonging to the private residence of the Sheriff. As to the Clerk, being a pious man, he of course learned humility. He sat upon the end of the puncheon bench assigned to the bar and kept his papers in his coat pocket. Whenever he wanted one, he had to look them all over.*[28]

Almost four years later, Gainesville got a new court house, which DeMorse applauded. It cost $300 with wood that had to be hauled from Jefferson. It had a door on each side of the building and two windows at each end. Talk about improvements!

> *The village of Gainesville which, when I was last at it, had four families for inhabitants, had increased in size and population. It has put aside somewhere the little log house without a floor and the cracks unstopped, which was of old the Palace of Justice and has erected in its place a respectable framed court house of dimensions sufficient for all present use.*[29] *The Town has three attorneys.*[30]

DeMorse showed no bias. He roundly criticized his hometown Clarksville's courthouse, calling it an "ancient time worn, weather beaten, dilapidated Temple of Justice, [which] has long been an eye sore to the Town and County."[31] He expressed his glee that it was to be sold to the highest bidder and carted off. An impatient DeMorse even suggested that "the boys got up an illumination" and burn it down.[32]

Stories have come down about some of the other early courthouses in Northern Texas. For example, the first court house in Grayson county, formed in 1846, reportedly was built at the cost of $232 by the citizens as part of a July barbeque, where two fiddlers played and a barrel of whiskey drunk. Legend has it that the first court house built in Sherman was torn down in 1858 to settle a bet whether a gray goose was nesting under its floor.[33] The story appears apocryphal. DeMorse provides us a first hand report. The building - or part of it - fell down under the weight of a large crowd listening to a case underway in the second floor court room.

> *The old Court here, a long two story wooded structure, upon a lot fronting the square, was put up without any girders to hold the sides together and generally in a frail mode. On the day I got here, the stairs leading to the second story fell down and seriously hurt one man. It is a wonder that many limbs were not broken. The stair were on the side of the house near the back; the Judge's seat was central to the back of the court room. Quite a number of people were sitting on the steps listening to the speech of some attorney and as number were under the stairs, also listening. So it seems strange that with weight of the people super added to the weight of the flight of steps, more of those underneath were not injured. The next day the wind being high the whole structure was so much affected by it that the joists [joints] on the floor above the courtroom, began to draw out of the mortices in the central girder in which they were rested and were held up at one end only by the nails, which held them to the second floor. This movement alarmed the court and it adjourned to the Church for the remainder of the week.*[34]

As time went on, the log courthouses gave way to framed ones, like those in Tarrant, Hopkins County, [a "neat two story frame court house, 30 by 40 feet"[35]] or Buchanan County ["a small framed building of one room, sufficient for the present accommodation of the auditory assembled at Court."[36]].

But the future was in brick, not wooden, courthouses. In 1847, although its old court house was, at worse, only two years old, Paris was so booming that another court house had to be built in the town square, the county's fifth. It would be of brick, the first in Texas. DeMorse gave it a mixed review to his readers:

> *Court House at Paris*
>
> *They are building at Paris, Lamar County, a brick court house, the walls of which are nearly completed. It is two stories high and would be an excellent building, but for the fact that it is not sufficiently elevated and that the stories are too low, the first being but ten feet and the second about eleven feet. The bricks are excellent and the workmanship of the wall of the best sort, as good as could be desired. The first story, however, should have been at least two feet higher from the ground and should have been between one and two feet higher between the floors and ceiling and the second story should be fourteen feet between floor and ceiling. This, with the quality of the building, would have made it a conspicuous ornament to the town. As it is, or as it is likely to be, it will only excite regret that so good material and workmanship have been used to so little advantage.*[37]

Several years later, when it came time for his own Red River County to replace its original log courthouse, DeMorse gave his views to the *Standard's* readers:

> *Our Court House. . . The County court will soon decide upon proposals for this building and determine upon its character. In this determination, price should not be the only consideration. Low price may not be*

cheapness. It is true economy to have good materials, well put together at fair prices, rather than poor materials, put up in an unworkmanlike manner, neither elegant in appearance or durable. We have waited a long time for a court house, are amply able to build one now and should have a good one. . . and should be satisfied with nothing less. A good court house can be put up only with first class workmen.[38]

The new court house in Clarksville was erected on the spot of the old one, that is, center stage, right in the middle of the Square, the most important building in Town. Built of brick, it was the first attempt in Clarksville to use this material,[39] cost ten thousand dollars, from soup to nuts, and took about six or seven months to complete. It was good sized, "45 by 55 feet with a base of three feet, a lower story of 12 feet to the ceiling, an upper story in which is to be the Courtroom, two clerks offices, 15 feet from floor to ceiling and these with the cornices will give the building an elevation of 33 feet. It is handsomely finished throughout, with seats for the audience. The walls are to be 18 inches thick."[40]

Inside and out, it was nicely appointed:

Our new court house is progressing rapidly to completion, the external painting is nicely and looks like nearly done. The painting of the courtroom is also nearly done and the carpenter's work for the Judge's seat, the Bar, the Jury seats and the Audience is finished and present a neat and commodious appearance. The seats for the audience rise from front to back so as to give all a view of the proceedings of the court.[41]

Soon, other counties followed Lamar's and Red River's examples, constructing their second generation courthouses of brick also. Grayson County's new courthouse in Sherman was a copy "in size and arrangement" as that in Red River." DeMorse thought it should be larger - at least 50 by 75 feet - because in five years it would be too small. He also opined that the clerk's office could been larger, less space be wasted in the passages, and the jury room be put upstairs.

As with the courthouses in other counties, the one in Grayson served many purposes. It was used for dances, sermons, shows and theater. Spreading a few inches of sawdust on the floor reduced wear on the floor. It certainly was a durable structure, lasting until May 9, 1930 when it was burned down by a lynch mob.[42]

DeMorse also reported on Dallas' new fifty foot square brick court house, built on the Square. He found some fault with it, of course:

> *The windows are too large proportionally for the size of the building, giving it a rather unsubstantial appearance. The top has a flat roof hidden entirely by a low parapet. The arrangement of rooms below is similar to our court house, being one at each corner of the house. Less space is wasted than in ours. The court room above occupies the entire square of the house with no room cut off for jury rooms as in ours.*[43]

In 1857, Hunt County's planned brick courthouse was to be smaller than Dallas - only forty feet square - and DeMorse, while saying "it is not quite so large as it should be" allowed that it would be "sufficient for a few years to come." The masonry and carpentry work was to be done by a contractor named L. W. Lissenbee, whom DeMorse endorsed "as a contractor who will not have bad work done."[44]

It seemed many of the counties were by 1860, either tearing down, soliciting bids for a new court house[45] or building it.[46]

The Texas frontier moved west at a steady pace and, as new counties were formed, the legal system was not far behind. By 1857, it was moving southwestward, past Cooke and Tarrant. The first court session in Gilmer drew over a hundred people, was held in one of the rooms of a two room house, which was one of two buildings in town. The other was "the unfailing attendant of all towns, however new, around which, were gathered those jovial spirits who worship the Jolly God and drink to time as it flies."[47]

Chapter Four

Judges of Northern Texas

For litigators - those who earn their livings in the courtroom in adversarial settings - there is little better than having a good judge or worse than having a bad one. It was probably doubly true for DeMorse and his comrades who rode the circuit with that particular judge for weeks on end.

In his two decades of reports on his travels, DeMorse provides us with snippets about some of his saddle mates, judges with whom he rode the wilds and before whom he appeared in court at the trek's end.

On DeMorse's "good judge" list was Judge John T. Mills. He appears to have been an extraordinarily capable judge and ethical attorney, respected by the bar and citizenry alike.

Born in Ireland in November 1817, Mills moved with his parents to Beaufort County, South Carolina. He studied law there and, in 1837, went west to Texas. He began his practice in Clarksville, home also to DeMorse and *The Standard.* He married Mary Jane Vining also of Clarksville in 1843.[48]

From 1839 to 1846 Mills sat as judge for the Third, Seventh, and Eighth Judicial districts. He had the reputation of moving his docket along.

> *The District Court which has been is session for the last two weeks, Hon. John T. Mills presiding, adjourned today. A large number of cases have been disposed of.*[49]

> *The District Court for this county adjourned on Saturday evening last, after a session of two weeks, in which more than one hundred cases were disposed of. Judge Mills still retains the high estimations our citizens awarded him, at the first circuit he made in this District, and dispatches business with a rapidity seldom surpassed.*[50]

He was certainly respected by his fellow members of the Bar and Bench.

> *Invitation to the Hon. John T. Mills by William C. Young, W.R. Scurry and B. H. Martin, on behalf of the Jurists Association of the Seventh Judicial District, to deliver an address "upon the character of [the legal] profession and the Duties of Attorneys" and his acceptance of the invitation.*[51]

Look at the following remarks published by the grand jury of Lamar county as it finished its term. Note also how the grand jury viewed itself as the "moral regulator of the community."

> *The Grand Jurors for the County of Lamar, having closed their investigations, cannot consent to return to their homes without giving expression of their sentiments of regard and esteem which they entertain for the Hon. John T. Mills, presiding judge.*
>
> *When they take into consideration the peculiar disadvantages under which this position of the Republic has heretofore labored for the irregular administration of the law having now assumed of a different, firm and consistent character and that order has been introduced throughout the legal organization of the county, concerning that this improvement has been induced by the capacity and conduct of the presiding judge, the expression of the fact and the acknowledgment of the benefit, is due to the truth highly creditable to him and pleasant to themselves, they therefore conclude by reassuring him of their high respect and regard for him, both as an officer and as a gentleman.*
>
> *The Grand Jury would tender to the District attorney, John Benton Jr., their thanks for his assistance throughout the investigations, his promptness in his official capacity and the courtesy of his demeanor during their intercourse.*
>
> *Having performed the duty as moral regulator of*

the community to the best of their abilities, they retire to their homes, conscious of the rectitude of their conduct and sincerely desiring that the result of their labors may prove beneficial to the community.

The Grand Jury desires that their presentation be filed among the records of the County and published in some newspaper of the country.[52]

On DeMorse's "worse judge" list was William Smith Todd. Born in Virginia, Todd was well educated and experienced: a graduate of University of Virginia and a two term legislator there. Around 1840, Todd and his family moved to Bowie County. Todd established a law practice and his wife Eliza Todd opened a school for wealthy young ladies girls, Ringwood Female Seminary. In 1848, they moved to Clarksville, where Todd continued to practice law and his wife opened the Clarksville Female Institute. She often advertised in *The Standard* and DeMorse was very complimentary of her and the school. Two years later, Todd was elected judge of the Eighth Judicial District and was reelected to two more four year terms.[53]

Something must have happened between him and DeMorse because DeMorse began to be very critical of the judge, normally not a prudent thing for an attorney to do to a judge before whom he regularly appears and travels. It began in 1859 when the Judge missed Court because of illness. At first, DeMorse was neither very critical nor sympathetic

There was no District Judge at Bowie this week and consequently no Court. Jurors, witnesses and others learned of the failure on Wednesday, by the arrival of F. S. Moseley, Esq. of Jefferson and, of course, scattered after receiving the information.[54]

Judge Todd wrote a letter to DeMorse referring to his inability to hold court, explaining:

I have had an operation performed on my right foot, from a disease from which I had suffered great

pain for more than two years and although I reached home in time to have served the Bowie Court, I was not able to walk on my foot and consequently was compelled to forego the pleasure of discharging my duty to the people of that county. If you think me entitled to the courtesy, I shall be pleased to see this explanation published in your paper

Respectfully yours,
W. S. Todd[55]

Apparently, Todd's illness and his missing Court continued and DeMorse finally objected to it in his newspaper. The Judge's absence affected the lawyers with long trips and wasted time, clogged the dockets for the next term and, most importantly, interfered with the lawyers' revenue stream. DeMorse's criticism of Todd's missing court resulted in a reprimand from another newspaper:

The Jefferson Herald reported that Judge Wm. S. Todd had returned home and would commence holding his court at Mt. Pleasant at the regular time. It also said that his prolonged absence was unavoidable and the greater part of it was occasioned by the feeble condition of his health. The remarks of the Clarksville Standard that the people of Bowie had been come somewhat used to doing without court were wholly uncalled for. It is true that Judge Todd has missed three consecutive spring courts in that county yet we presume the people of Bowie county are perfectly satisfied that the causes that lead to these failures were wholly unavoidable.[56]

To which, DeMorse replied by denying that the absences were unavoidable or the people of Bowie were satisfied:

The Judges of the State are paid to hold court at stated intervals and when their private business becomes so important as to interfere with the performances of the duties that the State has entrusted them to them, they have the right of the choice of service but they have no right to draw the money of the state for services which they do not perform - taking something for nothing, disappointing litigants who are entitled of right to their attention and disappointing officers of the court who have to live by their profession and have responsibilities which they cannot meet in consequence of the deliberate acts of the official, whose presence is essential to the accomplishment of their labors. No man has the right to accept the People's money and to neglect the services for which it is paid to him and, if the Chief Justices of counties do their duties, perhaps it will not be found profitable for District Judges to make their public duties secondary to their personal convenience. It is not alone the people of Bowie who have cause of complaint.[57]

Judge Todd's son, George T. Todd, a young lawyer[58] jumped into the fray to defend his father's honor and DeMorse took him on as well, warning him not to ask too much about his father because he may not end up happy with what he learned.

The young gentleman is operating under the delusion that the bar of the district is very anxious to retain his father's services. We would suggest to Mr. Todd that we have no wish to force any disagreeable knowledge upon him and that it would be very prudent of him not to push his personal investigations too far.[59]

Judge Todd retired from the bench at the end of his term because of his poor health and died two years later.

Sometimes, judges in Texas in the 1840s and 1850s had to be tough. In fact, a section of East Texas was known as the Neutral Ground[60] and acted as an uninhabited buffer zone between Spanish and Mexico Texas and the Unites States. But it soon became a *mecca* for settlers - in many instances fugitives from justice from both nations. They ignored the directions of their governments and settled there. Twice, in 1810 and in 1812, the two governments had to send in a joint expedition because the outlaws, who had flocked there, were disrupting trade and immigration.[61]

DeMorse began publishing *The Standard* in 1842, while this lawlessness was still rampant in the Neutral Ground and immediately was very outspoken against it. DeMorse was also angry that the residents of Harrison and Shelby counties reportedly were ignoring the Texas revenue agents and not paying taxes, understandably offensive to the citizens of Clarksville and Red River county who were paying their obligations.

> *The sickness of Judge Mills, who is still indisposed, prevented the session of the Court in Harrison County. It is unfortunate, for the peace and good name of the Republic, the collection of the Revenue, and the profile of the grave and venerable District Attorney, who had a fine field before him in that little rotten borough, that the Court was not held. We understand that, had there been a Court, the criminal docket would have been graced with some twenty beautiful little cases for murder, besides other graceful and popular employments in that region, such as defrauding the Government of its tax revenues.*[62]

Things got so bad there in 1844, with assassinations and lynchings, that President Houston had to lead a force of militia to the town of Marshall amid reports, circulated by DeMorse and likely erroneous, that "twenty four men had seated themselves on a log in town and said they would yield to no one but would sooner die, where they were. They were armed with two guns, or pairs of pistols, and a Bowie knife each. They were swearing vengeance against Sam Houston and Judge Miller, says our informant."[63]

DeMorse, usually not a fan of President Houston, applauded him this time for quelling those who had "run riot over law and public decency long enough."[64] The show of might at Marshall by the government, evidently worked.[65]

There was, however, an occasional relapse, like an

attempt to shoot the trial judge. DeMorse illustrates how busy criminal defense counsel were in Harrison during the clean up period.

> *Harrison County - From Marshall, we learn that the District Court has adjourned after a session of five weeks and the accomplishment of much business. We are assured that the session of the court and the practical evidence of the power of the laws has had a most beneficial tendency. As a general thing, everything has gone on quietly, although a little diversion, in the way of trying to shoot Judge Ochiltree, concluded the performance of the term, just enough to show that the old tricks are not forgotten. A fellow by the name of Neal, which some our citizens may recollect for flourishing around here with a double barreled shotgun, a month or two since . . . considered something done by the Judge to be an infringement upon his dignity or rights . . . went into his office on Saturday, after the adjournment of the Court, to shoot him, that being the approved practice under the Harrison Republican system. Manifesting his intention by sundry threats, General Henderson overheard him, stopped him at the door and told him he would shoot him if he moved any closer to the Judge, whereupon the Regulator walked off . . . Twenty two indictments for murder were found and forty odd for aggravated cases of assault with intent to kill, showing pretty clearly that there was a need for a Court.*[66]

Another tough Judge was John H. Reagan. Born in Tennessee in 1818, he had had little time for schooling. He worked with his father at a tannery and on their farm. In 1834 he attended Boyd's Creek Academy for fifteen months and, after taking off from school to earn some money for tuition, he spent another year at Southwestern Seminary. Drawn to Texas, as so many were, he quickly found himself fighting Indians in the Cherokee War. While working as a surveyor and frontier scout, Reagan studied to be an attorney and, in 1846, obtained a law license. He opened an office at Buffalo on the Trinity River and, when the judge of the Ninth Judicial District died, Reagan was popular enough to win a hastily called election. It was the first post he was to hold in an impressive list.[67]

DeMorse respected Judge Reagan as the following report from court in Dallas illustrates:

> *Tomorrow a numerous party, including the Judge and his young bride, start for Birdville the county seat for Tarrant County. I have now have been at two courts held by Judge Reagan and have intermixed with the Bar and the People. As the Judge is new in his position (and since every new position is in some degree a trial), I feel that it is only proper to say that he fills it with a modest dignity and courtesy of demeanor that cannot fail to make him very acceptable to the People who have elected him to his high station. Judge Reagan is a young man and has won his place in this community by study and perseverance. As he has a capacity and integrity and has risen by merit the is entitled to honorable consideration therefor.*[68]

An item from *The Standard* gives today's lawyer a glimpse of the dangers back then in being a judge, like Reagan.

> *Trouble in Kaufman county - A gentleman just in from Kaufman informs us that the county is in a state of open rebellion, and that serious difficulty is apprehended between a set of desperate characters, who reside there, and the legal authorities. Letters of a threatening nature have been addressed to Judge Reagan and the district attorney, warning them that, if they come into the county for the purpose of holding the next regular term of the court, that their lives will be taken. Some of those letters are anonymous and some are, we understand, from responsible men - one from the District Court Clerk.*
>
> *We know that Judge R. and the Prosecuting Attorney are men of too much nerve and personal courage to be deterred from following the strict line of their duty, by the threats of personal violence emanating*

from such a source and we cannot but believe that there are a sufficient number of law abiding citizens in Kaufman to protect the court in the discharge of it duties.[69]

One of Judge Reagan's law partners in his earlier days was Nathaniel Macon Burford. Tennessee born, he was a graduate of Irving College and the law school at Lebanon, Tennessee. He was admitted to the bar in 1845 and ended up in Cass county in January 1847. He became deputy clerk of the district court there, but found that the bar was too crowded for his career ambitions. He pushed on to Dallas in October 1848, with five dollars and several letters of recommendation. In Dallas he soon formed a law partnership with John H. Reagan and in 1850 and 1852 was elected district attorney. In the 1852 he became judge of the new Sixteenth Judicial District.[70]

DeMorse knew and road the circuit with Burford. As he sometimes did with other Judges[71], DeMorse bragged a bit how friendly he was with the Bench. "Tomorrow, in company with Judge Burford, whose guest I have been for the past two days, I start for Sherman."[72]

Judge Burford seemed willing to undergo a little inconvenience for the sake of dispensing justice. DeMorse recalls one session in Alton, then county seat of Denton county:

The district court has been in session here, Judge Burford presiding, since Monday morning. Court is held in an open log house without fire and the sessions during the cold weather prevalent during the week might be considered uncomfortable, but here, where a part of the attendants on the court sit up around log hearths because rooms cannot be had, no one grumbles much.[73]

Another of DeMorse's colleagues at the Bar who became a judge was Virginia born Bennett H. Martin. His parents emigrated to Kentucky but both soon died and the twenty one year old Martin took on the responsibility of raising his younger siblings. He had little formal education, and by trade, was a brick mason - that is, until he adopted the law as his profession. He came to Red River in 1844 and was given a certificate for 640 acres of land. He is listed in *The Standard* that same year as an attorney. The paper also showed him to be a candidate for brigadier general, Fourth Brigade, Texas Militia. He was named a judge of the huge Ninth Judicial District of Texas, then consisting of Grayson, Collin, Denton, Dallas, Kaufman, Henderson, Anderson, Houston, and Van Zandt counties. He later served as judge of the Sixth Judicial Court of Texas.[74]

Like so many of the members of the Bar in early Texas, Martin became involved in different public efforts whether it be coordinating the removal of obstructions to navigation of the rivers[75] to removing of another obstacle in the lives of Texas citizens - demon alcohol:

> *Temperance lecture. . .We are requested to state that Judge B. H. Martin will deliver a temperance lecture, at the Presbyterian Church, on Tuesday evening at candle light.*[76]

In 1852, *The Standard* sadly announced that "Judge B. H. Martin, formerly a citizen of this town, and lately Judge of the 9th Judicial District died on the 7th instant of typhoid fever."[77]

DeMorse crossed paths with many judges over his two decades of riding the circuit. Some we only know what DeMorse tells us about them. Judge E. H Ventress is an example. DeMorse pronounced. "He is a young man, but highly respected by the Bar and I have no doubt that he will be an honor to the station he occupies."[78] Gustavus A. Everts was another judge in the first decades of Texas. Born in Ohio, he immigrated to Texas in 1844. At the age of forty six, Judge Reagan made him district attorney for Dallas County in 1855. He later became a judge and road the circuit with DeMorse, who tells of the adventures and misadventures of one trip in April of 1853.[79]

The first report from McKinney in Collin county sets the scene:

Court will adjourn tomorrow morning (Saturday) and we shall separate, His Honor and the Clarksville members to the Cross Timbers of Denton and Judge Evans, Judge Everts, Reuben Eaves, Esq, the Knight of the Red Blanket and myself to Kaufman.[80]

A week later, DeMorse tells what happened on that trip to Kaufman.

Dear Sir: On Friday of last week the District having adjourned at McKinney, a company consisting of Judge Evans, Judge Everts, Judge Reeves, John E Cravens, Esq. and two others started for this place traveling down the East Fork of the Trinity River, 18 miles over a lovely prairie territory, to Wells Ferry, where we expected to cross. Arriving at the ferry at 3:00 o'clock in the afternoon, we found several gentlemen who had proceeded us and were awaiting the fall of the water. The creeks on both side of the river were overflown, and although there was a ferry flat at the river, there were none at the creeks and so we concluded to wait a few hours, as we were told that swimming the creek might be dangerous from Bois D'Arc brush in them full of thorns. So we waited to morning and the river rose during the night. This was not what we had bargained for and to make matters worse, the ferry man who had promised to haul a canoe and bring and put our saddle bags over dry, backed out and we returned on Saturday morning back to McKinney, all save Judge Everts and some citizens in the vicinity of Millwood who were not in a hurry.[81]

It would have been safer had Judge Everts stayed with the group:

Yesterday Judge E. who stayed at Wells Ferry waiting for the water to fall, got in after swimming all the creeks in the East Fork bottom. Traveling alone he saw an animal which he took to be a tiger and which he carefully went around. He had lost his way on getting here and at a small creek out of the way of travel, encountered the animal or rather saw it being peaceably disposed concluded not to encounter it. This is the second "varmint" seen in our travels. One of our company saw a wild cat in the tree on the way from Greenville to Bonham, in Bois D'Arc bottom.[82]

Two unpleasantries in being a judge is being reversed by the appellate courts and being underpaid by the legislature.

Regarding the former, *The Standard* published the surprisingly high reversal rate of the District Courts. For example, Todd had 23 reversed and 16 affirmed; Reagan was 29 reversed and 28 affirmed and Buford had 15 reversed and 10 affirmed. The least reversed judge was a Peter Gray with 10 reversed and 35 affirmed.[83] Of course, unlike today, filing an appeal and pursuing it in every case back then was not a knee jerk reaction to a loss.

As far as compensation for the Judiciary, it was a problem back then too. The private bar made a lot more than those on the bench. In one instance, an attempt was made at parity between Judge Burford and newer appointed judges, but it failed. DeMorse reported that a special law was submitted to the state legislature to increase the compensation of Judge Burford. The day after he was appointed, compensation for new judges went from $1,750 to $2,250. It was especially inequitable because Judge Burford "has to do more than any other District judge in the state." Forty two weeks a year he rode the circuit in his 16th District, which was very large - "bigger than many European principalities." DeMorse noted that there had been a bill to split the district in half but it got caught up in an unrelated legislative fight and not passed. The end result was that five new counties on the frontier were assigned to Burford as well. "He now goes as far as150 miles from home."[84]

Chapter Five

Texas Lawyers

There was no shortage of attorneys in early Texas, although none were native born or educated. They seemed to have immigrated in numbers disproportionate to their percentage of the general population. The majority was from the southern states. A few, like DeMorse, hailed from the North. Their educations varied. A handful, at most, attended a law school such as the law department of Cumberland University in Lebanon, Tennessee. Most, however, clerked or read the law in the offices of other lawyers who trained them in their profession. Some of the lawyers received undergraduate training at institutions ranging from Princeton to the Oneida Conference Seminary in New York. Some had little formal education. Bennett H. Martin, a well regarded member of the bar and later a Judge, was said to have the trade of brick and mason for the profession of the law.[85]

Sometimes how full a typical lawyer's life is best seen in his obituary. For example, the September 3, 1859 issue of *The Standard* reported on the death of Burrill P. Smith "from hemorrhage of the lung his residence in Sherman of Grayson County." The obituary reported that Smith was thirty four when he died, having been born in 1825 in Wilson County, Tennessee. He studied law at Murfreesborough, was admitted to the bar in 1845 and emigrated to Texas. He began his practice in Clarksville. Soon he was raising men and became a captain of a company in the War with Mexico, where he engaged in a number of battle. He was elected in 1849 by Red River voters to represent them in lower house in Austin. In 1851, he moved to Grayson with family and "was practicing law when he died."[86]

Two weeks later *The Standard* of September 17, 1859 reported on the death of Wm. M. Williams who had died at the age of 51 in Lamar county of congestive fever, after a brief illness of 8 days." The "Major", as he was called, was a

Virginian by birth, had emigrated to Texas in his early days, when it was still a part of Mexico. "Poor and friendless", he settled in what is now Lamar county, fought for independence from Mexico, was made one of the first district attorneys and was a member of both house and senate at various times.

As had Smith and Williams, many early North Texas lawyers dedicated part of their careers to the *res publica*, the public good, including representing indigent defendants. They also served as district or prosecuting attorneys, county clerks and members of the legislature. Some ran for office. John J. Good of Dallas became its first mayor. His law partner, John McClannahan Crockett became its second and, later Lieutenant Governor of Texas. DeMorse, himself, who had been Clarksville's first mayor, later would be nominated for Governor in 1873 and 1886.

There was something in the litigator that seeks battle beyond the court house. Texas lawyers left and fought in the Texas Revolution, the War against Mexico and, as we shall see, in the War between the States. Others like attorney Edward H. Tarrant was an able and enthusiastic Indian fighter.[87]

The Standard identifies many of the lawyers of Northern Texas (*see Appendix*), either in news accounts of court proceedings or by nearly two decades of their "professional" or business cards in the classified section of the paper. Between the two sources, a profile of the members of the Northern Texas Bar emerges. For example, we can confirm that the name lawyers give themselves is the same as today, typically "Attorney and Counselor at Law" or just "Attorney at Law." Occasionally, those wearing other hats added "U.S. Commissioner" or "General Land Agent" to their titles.

We can also glean from these business cards that all, but a very few, of the lawyers from 1842 through 1861, practiced in one of the county seats[88] of North Texas and had their offices on the public square. In fact, the locations of the lawyers' offices were sometimes provided on their card: "on the south west side of the Public Square" or "next door the District Clerk's" or "next to store of John S. Gordon" or even "upstairs in the Courthouse."

The cards also recited each attorney's speciality. For

litigators, that meant principally the courts in which they regularly practiced. During the Republic, when the population was in the eastern counties, it was easy. "Will attend all the District Courts in the Eastern portion of the Republic and the Supreme Court." But, with statehood, came even more settlers. Original counties were divided and re-divided. Red River county, for example, was to become thirty nine different counties. Almost every year, the frontier moved westward and new counties had to be created. Soon, the litigator's beat became more complicated to describe: "will practice in the 6th and 8th Judicial Districts; also in the Supreme and Federal Court at Tyler"; or "practices regularly in the District court of Collin, Grayson, Denton, Tarrant, Parker, Johnson, Ellis, Dallas and Kaufman counties and at the Supreme Court of the state."

Most of the lawyers were solo practitioners but there were some two or three man partnerships, like Williams, Milwee & Townes with offices in Grayson and Lamar or Gray and M'Kenney, which had attorneys resident in both Mt. Pleasant in Titus county and Tarrant in Hopkins.

All promised that they would be attentive to their clients needs and diligent in providing the services promised: "All business entrusted to his care shall have prompt attention"; "he has long resided in this portion of the State and flatters himself that the liberal patronage heretofore extended to him is a sufficient guarantee of his ability and prompt attention to business." References were often given as well. The Burford & Dyer firm of Dallas, for example listed Texas clients as well as some in Nashville and New Orleans. Wm. E. Wootten of Clarksville gave as his reference one of the best known churchmen in Texas, Rev J. W. P McKenzie, President of McKenzie Institute.

Among the traveling troupe of lawyers was the district or prosecution attorney who represented the People in criminal cases. One was Sumter R. G. Mills, who was the younger brother of Judge Mills. He had immigrated to Texas in 1856, was elected D.A. and then re-elected. But only three years later, at the age of 26, he had to resign because of bad health.[89] Two months later, *The Standard* reported that young Mills had died at his mother's house on Beach Island, South Carolina.[90]

Being a D.A. must have been a good post because within days of Mills' resignation , John C. Burks became a candidate for the job.[91] Within two weeks, Wm. Evans of Bonham, E. F. Estes and E.D. McKenney all threw their hats into the ring.[92]

Lawyers have thick skins, to ward off the blows of their adversaries and the public in general. Since Shakespeare's popular, but always misunderstood quote about "the first thing to kill all the lawyers"[93], attorneys - the wicked wags of law - have been the butt of a lot of jokes. DeMorse and *The Standard* continued it:

> *The London Inns of Court Rifle Volunteer Corps, which is entirely comprised of lawyers, have received a very good nick name "The Devils Own" and "Retained for the Defense" has been suggested a s a motto for them.*[94]

> *Why is Judge X like necessity? Because he knows no law?*[95]

> *A lawyer is a learned gentleman who rescues your estate from others and then keeps it for himself.* [96]

> *Winning a cat with the loss of a cow is what the Chinese call going to "Law."*[97]

An item from *The Standard* praised the "model town" in New Hampshire which "supports neither doctor, lawyer, clergyman nor pauper. It is one of the best farming towns in New Hampshire, has about 90 voters, many of whom are thrifty and wealthy farmers."[98] DeMorse himself added to the popular image of the lawyer who stirs up trouble on which he and his fellows could profit. In a visit to the just organized county court, DeMorse noted that there was not much activity and that "there were ten cases on the docket and twenty attorneys to feed upon them."[99]

Chapter Six

The Practice

What type of work did early Texas lawyers do? Has it ıanged much today?

Certainly, there was a civil side to the practice, both in ıe office and at court.

Real property law was popular. Immigration to Texas 'as heavy. Incoming settlers purchased or leased the farms of ıe pioneers, who themselves were moving westward with the ontier. Many of the first residents of the region held land :ants from Mexico or the Republic. Veterans had leagues of .nds given them by a grateful government. Others owned head ghts of land, originally granted them as inducements to settle. ome lost the certificates evidencing their ownership and had to ɔ to a lawyer to learn how to give notice and secure title.[100] In :her words, the real estate business was booming and lawyers 'ere needed to facilitate the transfer and make everything legal. gain the professional cards that DeMorse carried each week ı the back page of *The Standard* give us today a glimpse of ıat practice as well: "letters requesting information in regard Texas lands, title etc, when accompanied with a fee, will :ceive prompt attention"; "special attention given to collection f claims, investigation of land titles, writing deeds &c."; "he 'ill also act as agent for the purchase and sale of lands"; and ɔerfecting land titles, procuring patents to land, paying taxes ɔon land, redeeming lands sold for taxes, buying and selling .nds etc."

Of course, there is a litigation side of a real property :actice and *The Standard,* through the public notices it ıblished, gives some examples. One notice of trustee sale dvises the world that Henry Rhine is foreclosing on John nderson's lot in Clarksville; "a hundred feet west on Main reet of the southwest corner of a two acre lot that R. M. opkins had conveyed to Anderson."[101] There were other :tions for trespass. Some of the cases could be big like *Gen. T.*

land on the Trinity.[102]

The administration of estates provided much business to lawyers. When someone died, an administrator (or an executor if there were a will) was appointed by the court in the county where the decedent passed away. Notice was given by the fiduciary in a newspaper like *The Standard,* that all those indebted to the estate should make their identities known and pay off their obligations and that, similarly, all creditors of the estate should come forward and file their claims against the estate within the period proscribed by law, twelve months, or risk having their claims barred. De Morse, a lawyer himself, warned fiduciaries, that if they neglected to give this statutory notice, then they themselves would be responsible to pay late claims. This, of course, accounted for a great deal of business for *The Standard*, which was really the only newspaper in the region where that notice could be given.

Some types of practice have disappeared such as the law involving stray animals. First, notice was given: "Notice by C. S. Young, four miles east of Clarksville, that his horse has strayed or been stolen."[103] When a horse was found and unclaimed, there was another notice which told who found the horse, the two citizen appraisers who fixed a value to the stray and then the justice of the peace and his clerk who confirmed the appraisal.

There were some true specialities among members of the Bar, such as "securing business licences for those who want to trade with the Indian Nations", "perfecting and quieting titles to land"; "acting as a commissioner of deeds of other states for the acknowledgment of deeds and mortgages"; and " taxes, soldiers claims and claims against the state." There was even a bankruptcy practice in the state, that is, until Texas joined the Union. After that, of course, the Federal Courts, under the U.S. Constitution, had sole jurisdiction over bankruptcy.[104]

DeMorse's own professional card read:

CHARLES DE MORSE,
ATTORNEY AND COUNSELOR AT LAW,
Clarksville,
Will practice only in Criminal Cases and the collection of Foreign Debts. [105]

The trial lawyers did civil litigation. Collection work was common as were other types of cases familiar to lawyers today. They included suits for debt, for fraud, suits in equity, and divorce actions. Interesting, as in modern jurisprudence, the court obtained "jurisdiction" over a defendant no longer residing within the Judicial District by serving him or her by "publication" - that is, by a notice of the commencement of the lawsuit published in a newspaper a proscribed number of times. In other words, "long arm jurisdiction."

However, most reported were criminal cases, perhaps because they made better copy. DeMorse's reports of over twenty years, provide us today an image of justice being dispensed in the early west. Were trials conducted in saloons, posses formed to pursue bandits or a lynch mob taking the law into its own hands? Lawlessness seemed, at least in Hollywood, to go hand in hand with the frontier. In the very first days, that was not always true - that is, if we can believe what these folks say:

> *But most attractive of all, and differing from all elsewhere, was the fact that [a visitor] found the latch key to every cabin door hung upon the outside. There were no locks to the dwelling, or meat house, or corn crib; every comer was welcome to the primitive hospitality - cordial, not passive, hospitality. He noticed that no man feared robbery or wayside danger, but camped out anywhere that fuel could be found, turned his horse on the abundant grass, cooked his meat on a stick, and his hoecake in the ashes and that the little camp coffee pot behind his saddle, furnished him facility for an invigorating beverage.*[106]

For example, a tale of early Clarksville[107], speaks of a time, soon after 1836, when a horse was stolen from a farm just outside of town. This had never happened before. No crime of any nature had ever been reported. There were no laws; there was no sheriff; there was no jail. A "posse"[108] was formed, tracked down the thief, captured and brought him back to Clarksville. There, the town's leading residents, in the midst of what is today the Clarksville cemetery on West Washington Street were set to hang the thief from the branch of a blackjack oak tree. One citizen, Dr. George Gordon, however, made a plea for mercy, arguing a horse was not worth a man's life. Another countered with the question that, since they had no jail, they would have to turn the thief loose on the public, if he were not executed. A vote was taken among the large crowd that had formed. Those in favor of the execution stood on one side of the road, those opposed on the other. Two judges, astride a single horse, rode down the road, counting votes.

Most extraordinarily, women were permitted to vote in that election - arguably the first such exercise of the right of women suffrage in Texas. To a woman, the fairer sex voted on the side of mercy, as did a number of the men folk. The thief was turned lose, reportedly after being kicked by a disappointed executioner.[109]

As romantic a tale as it is, it was not illustrative of what was happening in other parts of early Texas. In fact, the settlers whom Texas first attracted, tough enough to survive in what was still a wild place, were not necessarily the most law abiding types.

As today, some of the wrongdoing was against property, other against persons. Examples of non violent crimes against property found on the dockets of the District Courts of Northern Texas run the gamut including a variety of fraudulent conducts: forgery, theft by deception[110], counterfeiting[111], smuggling[112] and fraudulent land titles[113]. The dearest asset lost to another's misrepresentations might be a maiden's virginity. While not a crime necessarily, it was considered a wrong under the law and DeMorse reports how the case of *Nall vs Russell* for seduction occupied a whole trial day and the jury brought in a verdict of $1,350.[114]

Some of the criminal cases are amusing:

Our subscribers in the neighboring counties had well been on their guard against a traveling pedlar, calling himself Lineburg, who sells bad jewelry, with a lottery privilege. His tricks have made it necessary for him to leave town this morning and to refund the money which he had received for his worthless jewelry.[115]

A few days ago a man came to town [Greenville] on foot and took lodging at Mr. Brown's inn. He arrived in the evening, deposited his budget and a short time after his arrival, in daylight, he stepped up to a rack at the public square and unhitched a horse belonging to a young man named Arnold and left for parts unknown. Mr. Arnold followed him but could not overtake him.[116]

The United States Mail was broken open and robbed on the mail route between Greenville in Hunt County and McKinney on Tuesday last by one James Robinson, Mail Rider.[117]

Every night can be held the reports of firearms upon the streets and the whooping or halloing of drunken men and to strangers and persons visiting the place, such operations are not calculated to make a favorable impression or give character abroad. We have a good jail for the purposes of keeping those transgress the laws and bid defiance to peace officers and a little bit more expense for improvements upon our streets collected for corporate Texas would not be a useless expenditure.[118]

There was the occasional arson as a notice from the *Dallas Herald* reported *via The Standard:*

We learn from S.A. Venters, Esq., County Clerk of Denton county, that the jail at Denton was burned a *few days ago. The act is supposed to be the work of an incendiary, as suspicious circumstances indicate it. The building was a two story house, the lower part of logs and the upper framed and was believed to be one of the strongest and best built jails in this section. It had only been complete about 3 or 4 months ago at a cost to the county of $2,699 and was vacant at the time being burned.*[119]

Jail breaks were not uncommon as a report from the *Bonham Era*, reprinted in *The Standard*, indicates:

> *Last Monday night all the prisoners in our jail escaped, by removing the floor and digging a passage through the ground under the sill. There were four - Roselle from Lamar county, confined for murder*[120]*; McDaniel, a quarter blood Cherokee, charged with assault with intent to kill; Wiley, who stole a blindman's mule; and Conway who was caught riding another man's mare. The sheriff and the posse were after them the next morning. When last heard, the prisoners were having a jolly time at a distillery seven miles north of town. The jail was considered perfectly secure but the rogues had tools furnished by some persons outside.*[121]

One would expect to hear that rustling was big in Texas and it was. Livestock, allowed to feed unattended in the lush pasture provided by Nature, proved a temptation to some. In the hierarchy of such crimes, hog theft was the least of it, but it could end you up in the penitentiary.[122] Cattle stealing was considered petit larceny and not treated much more harshly - a year in the penitentiary. This, of course, was before cattle became synonymous with Texas and "rustling" a major crime.

Horse stealing was a risk for anyone with a good looking piece of horse flesh that could be sold or traded easily a few towns distant, not unlike a popular car is today. Most issues of *The Standard* had at least one notice, often with a reward attached, for stolen horses.

THREE HUNDRED DOLLARS REWARD

Two fine horses were stolen out of my lot, six miles above the mouth of the Bois d' Arc, on the Choctaw side, on the night of the 11th instant.

One of the Mares is a beautiful iron gray, some sixteen hands high, in good order and has been run in Fannin County against one of the horses owned by the Harts. The other Mare is a red sorrel, about fifteen and a half hands high, and has also been used as a running horse. No brands recollected except a saddle mark. Both mares were seven years old this spring.

The rogues were white and were seen loitering about Mr. Bush's Ferry the day previous to the theft and stated that they were in my employ. The night they committed the theft, they crossed.

I will give the above reward for the rogues and the horses, if delivered at Fort Towson. I will give Fifty Dollars each for the Mares and Two Hundred Dollars for the thieves.

R. M. Jones[123]

Usually, the theft was the work of professionals. Sometimes, as previously noted, the perpetrator was a lone thief, like the one, reported by DeMorse, who, after arriving in town on foot and, reserving a room for the evening, cooly in broad daylight "stepped up to a rack at the public square and unhitched a horse" belonging to a young man and rode off.[124]

Other thefts were the work of organized gangs.[125] One that operated in the Denton area might have had as many as seventeen members, at least according to the five that were apprehended.

The Houston Telegraph, reprinted by DeMorse in *The Standard*, reported the quick arrest of a horse theft suspect in Austin, only a couple of days after the theft. It led to the confession that:

[H]e had stolen several horses [in the last two days] and made sale of them signing his name on the different bills of sale as Jno Johnson, William Moore

and Andrew Crissel. He says he has a wife and three children in Wharton county, and says that he has seven brothers, who are engaged in the same laudable business. He disposed of his equine possessions very promptly and at prices that suit purchasers, believing probably that "quick sales and small profits."[126]

The Houston Telegraph editorialized on the subject of the big business of horse thefts, which was reprinted by DeMorse:

> *But seriously, horse stealing is becoming quite common in Texas - almost as common as murder. It has been but a few weeks since a gang of these rogues were arrested at Liberty, having stolen horses and gambled all along from Victoria to this place. Such men should be punished to the extent of the law in a country like Texas, where stock of all kinds is necessarily permitted to go at large, with no protection save for the fine distinction between meum [mine] and tuum [yours].*[127]

Indians were also a constant threat to steal horses. They not only rode and traded them, they also thought horse meat to be quite tasty. Texas' Indian population, by the 1850s, had been confined on two reservations in North Central Texas. They sometimes strayed:

> *The people of Parker had an Indian speech from General Tarrant on the first day and quite a feeling for active movements against the Indians was stirred up. Provisions were subscribed and money and 39 men enrolled their names for the expedition on the 4th of July.*
>
> *A squad of 8 to 10 went off on Thursday to meet some men from Jack and to proceed to the lower reserve and demand four Indians who had been stealing horses and whom these mem were satisfied they had chased a few days since, while in possession of the stolen horses. They say they intend to have them or to have blood and,*

if they get them, they intended to hang them. The incidents upon which they predicate their demands for the Indians are these. They say that, when out a few days since, they pursued four Indians who had stolen horses and had pursued them so closely that the Indians left a pony. The Indians going over hills and then going over boggy ground, pushing their horses down steep creek banks, finally got away. The men took the pony and carried him into Jacksboro. The next day, the Indians came in and claimed the pony as theirs and acknowledged that they had been chased by white men the day previous. They were examined by another party of white men and allowed to leave. These men, my informants say, have considered the matter are satisfied after reflection and comparison of their facts, that these four were the very Indians that they pursued, have seen the sub agent of the Lower reserve, who agreed with them as to the guilt of the four Indians and agreed to surrender them.[128]

Arrest for horse theft required a preliminary hearing and a posting of bond.[129] Conviction usually brought a relatively long stretch in the penitentiary in Huntsville – sometimes as many as four years. In an 1861 item, DeMorse argued for a more drastic penalty. Undoubtedly a bit biased at the time - the back page of *The Standard* carried an advertisement the same day regarding the theft of his own three old stolen filly - DeMorse had no difficulty in advocating in print that only frequent lynchings would stop horse stealing.

We know of no work more efficacious for checking this work, as the immediate administration of Hemp, whenever the thief is found with the horse and the case is clear. We have always thought that the old law of the Republic was the best extant on this subject. That statute punished horse stealing with death. It is an offense so easy of accomplishment in this state, that Penitentiary punishment is not adequate to its prevention.[130]

Obnoxious as it is today, slaves were considered property before the War between the States and could be the subject of theft as well. Sometimes they were stolen to be resold; other times, abolitionists were responsible. In this item from the Civil War period, DeMorse seems to see a connection between the petty thieves and the Jayhawkers, a Kansas abolitionist movement.

> *Negro Stealing*
>
> *When in Paris last week we saw one of a squad of Texans, Bennet's company, sent by McCullough in pursuit of Negro thieves, who were running off Negroes from Mississippi to Texas to sell. They were finally overtaken near Waxahatchie we believe and stopped and the Negroes recovered. One of them is Isaac N. Miller, well known to then people of Fannin county, where he traded in ponies some years back and for a few months had a little drinkery at Bonham. He is quite an agreeable person but not entirely above suspicion. About two years ago, we think that it was established to the satisfaction of the district court that he had been hung in Arkansas for horse stealing. It appears that his doom has merely been protracted. He will doubtless stretch a rope when he gets to McCullough or before that.*
>
> *We understand that Jayhawkers are extensively engaged in the Negro running speculation.*[131]

There were violent crimes, of course. Some were minor:

> *A fellow named Mason was fined $300 "for drawing a knife upon Sheriff Hearn while in the performance of his duty. There were several convictions for misdemeanors and Wm. Powers upon a charge of assault with intent to kill, was found guilty of aggravated assault and fined $100.*[132]

Others, when all the smoke cleared, are more humorous

than ugly:

> *Mr. Samuel McDaniel, an old citizen of Bowie, while in his cups, shot and seriously wounded his wife last Saturday night. He was arraigned, but upon examination before Esq. Battle, the injured party objected to testifying against her "Liege Lord" and as there were no other witnesses, he was necessarily discharged.*[133]

Others were much more serious

> *Murderous assault*
>
> *From Tarrant, Hopkins county we learn that Joseph Leroy and Marseilles went late at night to an outbuilding occupied temporarily by one Richards, a carpenter, building a house for Mr. John Jackson, near by. Calling up Richards that they were from the country and had fruit trees for Mr. Jackson, they attacked him upon opening the door, knocking him down several times with bludgeons and finally when he got away from them, discharged pistols at him, fortunately missing him. Richards ran to the house of Mr. Matthews nearby and his assailants followed him but were kept off by Mr. Matthews. Richards was severely hurt, his scalp cut open to the bone in several palaces and his body badly bruised. Leroy and Marseilles are in custody and have to find bail of $1,500 each or go to jail.*[134]

> *Assault with Intent to Kill*
>
> *On last Monday an Indian engaged in picking cotton for Dr. Ellet, while under the influence of liquor, attempted to kill his wife by stabbing her in the breast and dangerously wounding her. After committing the deeds he fled and pursued by dogs overtaken and brought to this place, Clarksville. He underwent examination before D. K. Jamison, Esq. and he was bound over in the sum of $2,000 and confined in the County Jail, to remain until tried by the District*

Court.[135]

An insurrection among slaves is a continuous fear in a slave owning society, which had to be punished immediately and without mercy. It did not make any difference if the master were an Indian or that it happened in the nearby Indian Territory. Note the brutality of the retribution exacted, especially on the accomplice.

> *Murder in the Choctaw Nation*
>
> *We learn from Walter Spencer, Esq. that Mr. Richard Harkins, a respected half breed Choctaw, residing opposite this county, was killed by a Negro man of his own on the 28th ult, at his place. Riding up to where the Negro man was splitting rails, the Negro asked him to assist in turning a log, and as Mr. Harkins stooped to do this, he struck him over the head with an axe and hid his body in a tree top till night, when assisted by a Negro woman who was in the plot, he packed a large stone and both assisting, the body was sunk in the river.*
>
> *On the Saturday following the Negro man was suspected and arrested and, after being whipped, confessed and took two Harkins and Mr. Fulsom, who were investigating the matter, to the river to show them where the body was sunk. While the two Harkins were endeavoring to raise the body, the Negro sprang into the river, refused all assistance and drowned himself. His body was recovered and placed on a pile of brush with the Negro woman and burned.*
>
> *The Negro woman and man were the property of Mrs. Harkins, a daughter of Col. Pitchlynn and the reason they give for the murder is that they thought if they killed their master the mistress would go back to her father and take them with her. They had, it is so said, no supposable grounds for ill will to Mr. Harkins, who was a most indulgent master, never whipping his slaves and never exacting any hard labor from them.*[136]

The motives for a slave killing a master varied and did not seem to include any attempt at securing their personal liberty. Sometimes, slaves killed their masters for their money. In Boston, Bowie County, for example, two slaves, George and Edward, were arrested for the murder of Col. Stephen Tickell in his bed as he slept. It was rumored that thousands of dollars in gold were kept hidden in the house. They confessed, turning over some of the money. A suspicion lurked that they had been put up to it by some white men who had the balance.

Sometimes, the murder came about as a result of a slave getting into an argument with an overseer. This happened across the Red River in Arkansas when "Mr Crabtree [was] hit in the head with a hoe, killing him on the spot."[137]

Some motives were bizarre. When a six year old Fannin county boy was found drowned in only a few inches of water, suspicion fell upon a slave woman in whose care the child had been placed that morning. After questioning, "she acknowledged that she strangled the boy and threw him in the water a few yards from where he had been found. The motive for her conduct was that some statement made by the boy to his mother a few days before had caused the Negro's own boy to be whipped."[138]

Whatever the motive for a slave killing a white person, the end result was always the same: death. The slaves in Boston, for example, were properly tried, convicted and hung. A mob took the slave that had killed the Overseer and, "without Judge or Jury put him on a mule marched him [across the Red River] to this side of the Texas line and hung him."[139] As to the killer of the child, "after consultation among the citizens, a Jury of Inquest was held, evidence was received, conclusively making out a case of murder and the woman was hanged."[140]

The citizens of North Texas came to the execution with some expectation that the wrongdoer would confess his guilt and ask forgiveness and that the observers would act as civilized adults. Not considered, apparently in the following instance, was that it took the prisoners twenty five minutes to die because the noose did act property.

Execution of the Negro Boy Peter

This boy, about 16 years of age, found guilty of the murder of his mistress, Mrs. Valentine was hung in the woods near town, yesterday evening about 2:o'clock. The boy asserted to the last minute that he had been induced it by a fellow servant to murder his mistress, an assertion we think that no one believes. He did not manifest as we thought any proper appreciation of his position and evinced no great terror. When dropped, by the withdrawal of the scaffolding beneath, he fell about a foot and died without any great struggle, although the running knot did not slip and the pressure of the rope was confined to the front and sides of the neck. He was apparently dead in 25 minutes. There was a gathering of spectators not so numerous as was expected and no unseemly demonstrations upon the part of any of them. A decorous dignity pervaded all who witnessed the scene.[141]

DeMorse, although an officer of the Court, believed that vigilante justice - the application of the "Lynch Law" as he called it - was sometimes necessary. Reporting on a murder in Navarro county, DeMorse argued that, unless these crimes were more vigorously prosecuted and the defense of self defense accepted less by jurors, then morally justifiable private vengeance would follow:

Murders would not often occur anywhere in the State, if they were properly punished, but as long as the jurors of the country avoid their duty and give license to crime by acquitting its perpetrators, just so long we may expect frequent recurrences of these acts which are so shocking to humanity and degrading to any people, who pass them by unpunished.

We see the termination which must come to pass, if proper legal retribution cannot be obtained. After a while, citizens will be slain who will be avenged by Lynch law and by deliberate acts of private vengeance, and we hold any man morally guiltless, who after his brother or father or some dear relative has been slain, and there has been a criminal avoidance of punishment by the executors of the law. We hold the man who for himself deliberately and cooly avenges his kinsman, morally guiltless. Society organized by law owes protection to each member who has yielded something of his personal rights to cement that society and, if it fails to protect him, his original rights revert to himself and he may properly protect himself and those and those who have a natural claim upon him for their protection. It is lamentable morally, but there is no doubt that in some parts of our country the jurors criminally fail in the in the performance of their duty and allow a false sympathy for the criminal rather than a proper sympathy for the victim to sway their verdict, in defiance of the law and of their sworn obligation.[142]

In fact, it is surprising to see how casually DeMorse treated some legal shortcuts at which today's Bar would be aghast. For example, in 1844, DeMorse reported on a "a small operation, in the way of hanging up a few repeats, was performed on the south side of South Sulphur, in Fannin county, about two miles from the line between Fannin and Lamar, on the 10th inst." Those hung were four white men who "murder[ed] some friendly Indians, believed to be Caddos, whom they visited under pretense of friendship." They also had stolen horses and slaves. One of the Indians killed "was a small boy who ran to the attacking party seeking mercy and was held up at arms length by one of the outlaws, while another (Mitchell) deliberately killed him with his knife."[143]

Despite the defendants not being brought to the traditional trial and not having any appeal, they did nonetheless enjoy more than a modicum of due process:

Somewhere about two hundred persons were present at the examination and execution of these men, whose names were taken down. A committee of four or six men were appointed by the persons present, and they elected a jury of twelve men to try the prisoners, giving the prisoners the right to object to any or all of the jury. Evidence was brought to show the guilt of the accused. Jones, White, Wray and Mitchell were convicted of murder and sentenced to be hung the next day.[144]

The condemned accepted their fates differently. One "told his wife who was present that he had expected this for the last six years and that he considered his arrest a providential event by which the lives of at least four more men had been saved. He commenced praying and preparing for death and said finally that he believed he was going to a better world." On the other hand, another of them "was perfectly hardened and indifferent to his death."[145]

Court houses, lawyers, judges and cases make up much, but not all of, the criminal justice system. It is the everyday citizen, of course, who is the plaintiff or defendant to the civil suits, the accused in criminal cases, and witnesses and jurors in both.

DeMorse occasionally commented on the civil spirit of some of the communities he visited. For example, in 1853, he reported that the citizens of Kaufman county were peaceful folk by and large, as "the Grand Jury found no Bills for offenses against the laws, which argues very good conduct of the people of Kaufman of the last six months."[146] He was impressed by the honesty of some people, even if they came from outside of Texas:

Mr. Samuel Rhine passed through this place last Saturday last and on his way to Jefferson, and while traveling through the Sulphur Bottom lost a package out of his pocket containing about $1800. After he had crossed the Sulphur, he missed the money and to use his own remarks it "made him lose his appetite." He retraced his way back to this place without hearing or finding his money; but on yesterday a stranger rolled into town inquiring for the owner of the missing funds and on being introduced to Mr. Samuel Rhine, delivered up the money all right. Mr. Rhine very generously made him a present of $50. The man's name is Levi Rollins, *hailing from Franklin county, Alabama.*[147]

Perhaps, justice, while more primitive in some ways than back East, was faster on the frontier.

> *The Red River District Court opened on Monday of last week. The case of the State vs. Jacob Shumacher charged with murder was given to the jury without argument and without leaving their chairs they returned a verdict of acquittal.*[148]

Sometimes it was fairer as well. For example, DeMorse's initial assessment of the intelligence of the citizens of Wise - for having subscribed to *The Standard* - appears to have been borne out at the first court session in that county that DeMorse attended. At least, if not their intelligence, then their sense of fairness in a murder case brought against two slaves:

> *There seems to be a considerable disposition among the people of Wise county to see that justice was administered to all who came knocking at the door. Judge E. H. Ventress presided. He is a young man, but highly respected by the Bar and I have no doubt that he will be an honor to the station he occupies*
>
> *The most exciting case that came up was that of the state against Martin and Clara, Slaves, for murder. The case was one that caused much excitement in Wise. The case came on. The State announced itself ready, so did the attorney for the defendants and the witnesses were put under rule. The State most singularly failed to make out the slightest presumption. Defendant introduced no evidence, the Judge gave the jury the law, the Jury retired for a few minutes and returned with a verdict of not guilty.*[149]

Johnson, too, was a frontier society, where the peace could only be kept by arms and the moral conduct of the majority. Witness DeMorse's assessment of the morality of the people of Johnson county. In it, we may glimpse the real reason why the county seat was moved from Wardville to Buchanan.

> *The business of the court terminated this morning. A Grand Jury of the best citizens was unable to find but four bills this term. This shows a good present state of morality. In years gone by, this county had some rough and bad population. At Wardville, five miles down Noland River, the old county seat, quarter horse raising and its attendant swindlings, were the only occupations of the inhabitants of the town and a large number of citizens of the county. It was kept up for months together, ceasing only when it rained. Wardville is now an extinct city and the pleasure loving crowd that frequented it, now scattered. I observe here, however, that very considerable number of people, more than I have seen in five years, openly wear arms. Making mention of it, I was told that they were a distinct class and were rapidly giving way to the progress of settlement.*[150]

Chapter Seven

Life on the Road

Trying cases out of town is an experience which modern litigators know all too well: airport delays, long drives, disappointing hotels with unfamiliar beds and poor food. Charles DeMorse and his colleagues of the Texas Bar of the 1840s and 1850s shared similar difficulties as they criss - crossed the Red River District. How did they cope? Items from *The Standard* provide Texas lawyers of today with some examples of life on the road back then. Let them decide which was the more difficult practice – then or now.

Getting there is half the fun?

Travel conditions today can sometimes be unpleasant, causing delays and inconvenience. Bad weather in the 1850s could be equally distasteful, even often dangerous. DeMorse reflected - somewhat philosophically - on one such unpleasant incident:

> *It rained upon us furiously all day and, a little before night, we swam a creek on our horses. Just before dark, we were near here [Gainesville], but our directions had given out. It was so cloudy that we could not see well and, getting to a creek just after dark and dubious about pursuing the road on the outside of the settlements, where houses are 15 miles apart, aside from the five farms clustered together here, we concluded to lie down and wait for light.*
>
> *As everything was very wet, we could not make a fire to dry our blankets or clothes. Getting up about 2 o'clock, we came on in the moonlight to within a mile and a half of this place, hobbled our horses and lay down again to wait for day. At dawn of day, we saddled*

again and were able to see the bluffs of the river. Pressing on we soon got into the settlement and found a warm breakfast agreeable, after a fast of 24 hours.

After an adventure of this sort, one is a capable of appreciating comfortable quarters, smoking food and a large fire. To enjoy life to the utmost, one must partake of some of the disagreeables as to appreciate keenly by contrast.[151]

Deluges of rain from spring time storms, today a harbinger of tornados, were a seasonal obstacle. The ground turned into mud, "[a] black waxy soil rolling up the sides of one's boots, until the pedestrian is compelled with a jerk of his foot every few yards to free himself from the weight which clogs his movements."[152]

Left Bonham on Friday morning, the clouds looking ominous of rain, which after we had gotten four miles from town let down it contents, not very gently. The thunder rolled heavily and the lighting flashed vividly in front of us. We kept on, until one sharp, quick crash, like a simultaneous discharge of a heavy pack of artillery, frightened all of our horses and that of the Judge, so much that he run off with him and could not be checked for some distance. The rain coming down more steadily after the startling peal, we halted at a farm by the road side for some hours, and in the evening proceeded four miles further to the farm of Mr. Zachary, ten miles from Bonham, where we got just before the rain again came furiously down. Here we were entertained hospitably and comfortably until the next day, when we started again, and getting down to the Bois D'Arc Creek and found it swimming. It had been during the course of the previous night out of its banks. Passing up 2 and ½ miles, we found a good ford and crossed.[153]

The spring rains, especially the downpours, made the rivers overflow and perilous to cross. A pair of adventures encountered at swollen rivers and creeks by DeMorse and the other members of the bar as they traveled from county seat to county seat, reveal the downright lousy side of *going to court in Texas*:

> *Dear Sir: On Friday of last week the District Court having adjourned at McKinney, a company consisting of Judge Evans, Judge Everts, Judge Reeves*[154]*, John E. Cravens, Esq. and two others started for this place, traveling down the East Fork of the Trinity River 18 miles over a lovely prairie territory, to Wells Ferry, where we expected to cross. Arriving at the ferry at 3:00 o'clock in the afternoon, we found several gentlemen who had proceeded us and were awaiting the fall of the water. The creeks on both side of the river were overflown, and although there was a ferry flat at the river, there were none at the creeks and so we concluded to wait a few hours, as we were told that swimming the creek might be dangerous from Bois D'Arc brush in them full of thorns. So we waited until morning and the river rose during the night. This was not what we had bargained for and to make matters worse, the ferry man who had promised to haul a canoe and bring and put our saddle bags over dry, backed out and we returned on Saturday morning back to McKinney, all, save Judge Everts and some citizens in the vicinity of Millwood who were not in a hurry. After dinner, we crossed the east Fork on the bridge and took down to a trail way crossing of Sister Grove Creek, which we swam our horses across and over which we walked with our saddle bags over a log. It was a rich damp sickly looking region and the banks were very muddy.*[155]

> *We mentioned the excess of rain. The Sulphur and Creek bottoms have been flooded.*
>
> *We started for Titus courts on Sunday morning the 13th instant, to go by way of Becknell's Bridge, and after riding through the rain nearly all day, and the*

weather rapidly changing to severe cold, we stopped with some members of the Bar at Wm. Humphreys, this side of Mustang Creek. We had swum the creek in getting there and our information had led us to believe that Sulphur and Mustang bottom would both be swimming and, as we have said, it was getting very cold. Next morning Mr. Humphreys told us that crossing the Sulphur was impracticable, as it had rained hard all night, and we turned back, having to go six miles out of our way to get home again and finding Ward's Creek Bottom overflowed. On Tuesday morning, we started with another gentleman, by way of Stevenson's Ferry and got there before the main rise did, and found the bank on this side still uncovered with water. The other side had overflowed but not so deep that our horses could not wade through, from the bank of the river. On our return, we tried the Bridge route again and, having a pilot, we got through the overflowed bottom, without swimming, although the water in two or three places was nearly up to the tops of our horses backs. We found the "terrible Mustang" dead low and crossable on foot, though the day after, it was high again. At Fulbright's little creek, we had to swim our horses and walk over the foot log with our saddle bags. At Ward's Creek bottom, we found from 18 inches to four feet deep, barely escaping swimming in three places, before getting to the bridge. For the first time too in our experience, we found the entire bottom of Robbins Creek under water and, although it had fallen some inches, when we got there, it was nearly swimming in one low place in it. Every little prairie drain between there and Town was in the same situation, so that our trip was rather a disagreeable one.

The members of the Clarksville Bar generally, though most of them have a strong inclination to cold water, have had rather an excess of it lately. Another member who started on Sunday alone, a few hours behind the first party, found McKenzie creek, five miles from Town, high up its banks, and in going in on his horse, was borne down stream about fifty yards before he could find any getting out place. Starting again towards Stevenson's Ferry, a little after the first party, he was stopped again by a creek, this side of Kickapoo and returned.[156]

Another time, with the Sulphur swollen two miles across, the traveling party had an adventure that triggered DeMorse's imagination. He contemplated how the scene - the Judge, District Attorney and lawyers, all trying to find a good ford to swim their horse across, would strike an Easterner. He summed it up with the phrase "Going to Court in Texas."

> *The editor returns late from Mount Pleasant making around about course of two days travel to overcome 31 miles direct, the beautiful stream with the ominous name, which intervenes between the two places being swimming in the bottom and preventing the arrival of the mail since Tuesday of last week.*
>
> *On Sunday last, the traveling company composed of the District Judge, District Attorney, sundry legal gentleman, an editor of newspaper in Northern Texas and some chance companions started for Becknell's Bridge over Sulphur, and after listening to interesting reports as to its capacity for swimming horses, on either side of the bridge, we at last arrived at McCory's on this side of the raging stream, and taking Mc along with us as a pilot, we disengaged our martingals and prepared to swim. At McCrory, we found a citizen of Titus, with a nephew in company, a small boy who had rode thus far on a pony. But the pony was too low for the depth of the river and the uncle took the boy up behind him, got McCrory to lead the pony and we all started in together in a line, including two dogs who swam in after us, and one of whom went through. The distance before us was two miles - a sea of water, affording an eminent probability of swimming whenever we came to the sloughs. As we entered the water, an enterprise most of us had gotten through*

before, the singularity with such an order of travel would strike a stranger impressed itself upon our mind and what a capital plate for a magazine would be a truthful delineation of our party passing through the watery forest, making up a scene of "Going to Court in Texas." We knew our guide knew the bottom as well as when it was under water as dry and as he said he did not believe that we had to swim, we calculated on only an occasional brush and went on in good heart. The water came high up our horses, directly after going in, and legs had to be held well up the sides of the horses to keep dry. The dogs who came in howled seriously and occasionally rested on floating limbs. But we got over dry and unhurt save for a few who plunged their feet sullenly into the stirrups and wet them and paid for it.[157]

Often, the wisest course is to surrender to the inevitable and end up being tardy for court. At least, the judge, who was with the party, would also be late:

> *My last was written at Greenville during the prevalence of a rain, which lasted until Sunday and rendered traveling too uncomfortable to be performed, except under the requirement of stern necessity. Having choice books on hand and some magazines, we passed the time pleasantly enough, in comfortable quarters, in the Greenville Inn, until Monday morning when the Sun shone upon us once more, after five days exclusion and we headed for Bonham.*[158]

Sometimes, DeMorse and his group got lost. Roads were not direct and, as new counties were formed, many of their trips were for the first time. Once, they got lost closer to home, halfway between Greenville in Hunt county and Bonham in Fannin. DeMorse blamed one of his companions, an unnamed attorney from Titus county. He referred to him as KN, which were not his initials but an indication he was a member of the nativist Know Nothing Movement[159], which DeMorse ridiculed:

The country between Greenville and Bonham midway is sparsely settled and offers a variety of roads. The selection of a route of late has become a matter of taste. Some prefer going directly, some from an ambiguity or tendency or a love of scenery or topographical surveying capacity, always take the wrong road, or at least the longest road between the two towns; and in this case following the District Attorney and a distinguished KN from Titus county and keeping no look out myself, I was surprised at noting a familiar road passing between the forks of Sulphur to find myself taking the route eastward rather than north. Getting directions from some Negroes nearby, we made for a different point on the compass and got to our destination in good time with a loss or 4 or 5 miles. I note this fact to show that certain natural tendencies may run in traveling the road, as well as traveling a political course. Once before attempting to make the same journey in the buggy of a distinguished KN, who insisted upon us riding behind his ponies, he took precisely the same course out of the true route, could not be persuaded, and after being put back on the true courser for Bonham after three or for miles, took out again.

Our experience of the topographical surveys under KN guides is quiet sufficient. The next time we travel from Greenville to Bonham, we will eschew KN [and] lead the way our self.[160]

December 1859 was snowy. DeMorse and his group ran into a snow storm as they rode to Bonham, when "the sleet changed to a veritable snow and the depth much greater, say 3 or 4 inches."[161] DeMorse even reported "one sleigh being driven about in enjoyment of the unusual past time." [162] The weather has not improved much when, after court in Bonham. DeMorse, was philosophical about it:

Our ride to Lamar commenced on Sunday afternoon the 18th in a rain and concluded on Monday about 2:00 pm in a snow storm. We met only the stage, and one man in a buggy with a blanket drawn over his head, who inquired whether this was not rather inclement weather. We expressed our conviction that it was rather - about fit for the Arctic regions. However, it was a variety of weather and variety is said to be the spice of life, so we did not complain. If one were never cold, he could not appreciate the comfort of a bright fire, which is the most genial invention imaginable at fitting times.[163]

Where to stay, what to eat ?

Much of the population in Northern Texas during the 1850s was on the move. Some were immigrants on their way west or looking around locally for a farm or business to buy. Others were folks, like DeMorse, whose professions took them from town to town. Usually, there would be one or two hotels and boarding houses in each town, the older, more established towns having the better ones. George Wright's advertisement of his Lamar Hotel in county seat Paris, is illustrative of the effort to lure the traveling public.

The Undersigned would respectfully inform his friends throughout the Red River District and the traveling community generally that he has just opened a House of Public Entertainment, in Paris, Lamar County, where he will be happy to serve all who may favor him with a call. His buildings are all new, large and commodious. His table will be furnished with the best the country affords. His stable, supplied with plenty of Corn, Hay and Fodder, are careful and attentive hostlers and charges moderate, every exertion made to afford entire satisfaction to those who may patronize his House.[164]

A monthly stay typically cost "$12 with lodging, $10 without." A night stay's for a man and his horse was a dollar and a half. A single meal for the man was forty cents, for the horse thirty five cents.

When there was a choice of lodging, then the personality and attentiveness of the host and hostess became a selling point. For example, the owner of the Howeth House in Gainesville was described as "an old Texan, a good Christian and a Prohibitionist, besides being a man of pleasant manner- four decided recommendations."[165] The Crutchfield House, in Dallas, which DeMorse allowed usually "set an excellent table" was well known for its "courteous and attentive host and hostess."[166] The Anderson House in Grayson, DeMorse wrote "has for its landlord an agreeable gentlemen, who attends to the comfort, provides well and responds promptly to all hints by them of anything desired for their comfort. The amiable land lady gives close personal attendance to the internal economy of the establishment and there is an evident determination of the part of both, to do all they can to merit custom."[167]

Even a new town like Jefferson, then the county seat for Cass county (and now for Marion County) had two hotels. Each had a different, albeit interesting personality. Both, DeMorse pronounced, were "well kept." The proprietor of one was a medical doctor, who had "thrown physic to the dogs" and assumed "the more gentlemanly employment of fattening and exhilarating the inner man, instead of nauseating and depleting the system."[168] His competitor kept an inn that was "a large and commodious establishment, with pleasant evidences of taste, rare shrubs and flowers which greeted the eye and refreshed the senses."[169]

The absence of good food on the road can add to the misery of being away from home. Fortunately, the hotels of North Texas provided some interesting victuals to the visiting lawyers. For example, according to DeMorse, antelope, served at the Howeth House in Gainesville, Hunt County "tastes very much like wild duck which has first been roasted and then made into a hash."[170] In Fort Worth, then still a military outpost, DeMorse and the other lawyers "were agreeably entertained" by the Commandant, Major Merrill and his staff. There they were introduced to a "refreshment concocted primarily of Champagne, which he assured us was the latest invention at the

St. Nicholas [a fashionable New York City hotel]."[171]

Often the band of attorneys sought lodging at the homes of private citizens. A Tarrant county "frontiersman" whom DeMorse described as "genial, humorous and his eye very fine" is a case in point. He also had a big house and a good house keeper to preside over it and, DeMorse, writes "we fared well, had good beds spread in front of the fire, plenty of venison, bear meat, pork, milk, butter and honey and the best corn bread I ever found anywhere."[172] DeMorse, for example, also fared well one rainy day by the fire at the home of Col. Mitchell's in Navarro county. And why not? The Colonel had a "good cook", a garden that yielded "the first growth of the Spring, some of the largest finest flavored radishes" that Demorse had ever eaten and hunters who brought in fresh game from the shores of the Trinity River. A satisfied DeMorse conceded that "although the eatables were not served up in courses or with much parade, they were not hard to put up with."[173]

The description in an advertisement in *The Standard* classifieds for the sale of the Union House in Bowie county an idea of what the hotel looked like:

> *House is large and commodious; two stories, 80 foot front with back building at each end and has a piazza to both stories at front. The property includes the main building, out buildings, furniture, 19 and ½ town lots and 150 acres of land within the limits of the corporation. Will be sold at a bargain.*
>
> *C.M. Waddill*[174]

As today, a good night's sleep is crucial to the next day's performance. Thus, overnight accommodations were always of concern to the traveler. Some towns, especially the new ones, did not have enough places to sleep all the visitors during court week. There were more visitors than there was room inside for visiting counsel at Alton, the original county seat of Denton County. But those, who did not have a room, seemed to have made the best of it:

> *The accommodations we have found this court is*

an improvement on the hard old times we has seen in this county. It is only a year and a half since, at the fall term in Alton, the weather was very cold, a large number of people had to sit up all night, by a camp fire in front of the hotel, because the house that fed them well enough was not sufficiently capacious to give them lodging. I have a precise and particular knowledge, visual and auricular, that night after night during nearly an entire week, they sat up and drank and sang, and then in the day time went about like others, who had slept. How they stood it for days and nights, without rest, has to be at this time an unsatisfied wonder to me. But I know that they did and I have seen some of the same wide awake stock here, this court, but resting now like other humans.[175]

Gradually, things got better. For example, the Anderson house in Grayson was praised by DeMorse as being "of good size, with rooms of ample size and plenty of fireplaces (usually deficient)."[176] Tarrant, he wrote, "has materially improved in one respect. It has a good hotel which with extra rooms especially engaged for the term of the court furnished all the guests with most comfortable sleeping accommodations."[177]

Transportation from town to town was by horse so the visiting attorneys were careful as to the attention given their steeds. Anderson in Grayson was said to have "a large and well furnished stable attached to his house [where] the traveler can see his horse well fed and groomed."[178] DeMorse praised the Crutchfield House in Dallas as having "the best stable I have ever seen in the state."[179]

Sometimes, the lawyers had to eat a modest meal on the road, in the wilderness, "a wayside dinner of one biscuit, one small piece of bacon and two boiled potatoes, with a supply of distilled milk, which sometimes helps wonderfully."[180] At other times, however, such a roadside repast could be positively delightful. A picnic! Imagine the scene when DeMorse and five peers, two of whom, an ex- Secretary of State and a member of the Legislature, rode together on a mail wagon, stopped for a quick bite while en route from Bonham to

McKinney:

> *There was swift wind blowing as we started over the high and beautiful prairie, but, save that it interfered with the broad rims of some of our hats, it did not materially lessen our comfort.*
>
> *At 12 noon we arrived at Pilot Grove Creek, a small rapid running stream that empties into the East Fork of the Trinity and here coming to a halt, before I dismounted, the ex-secretary had jumped out of the mail wagon and commenced to gather dry brush, a movement I did not immediately comprehend. With the brisk air of an old camper, however, he deposited it in the hollow of a blackened stump, one half of which had been burned off, and lighting a match and starting a fire in the brush soon brought forth a small coffee pot and doubt died away in the pleasurable expectation of a comfortable pot of coffee, which, on the road on a windy day, ministers vastly to the comfort of the inner man. Ours was no abbreviated luxury, for the ex-Secretary, versed in all the excellencies of gastronomy, placing his pot, filled from the fast running stream besides us, upon a quick fire which he had kindled, soon produced a tin box, within which was ground coffee mixed with egg, the contents of which were carefully stirred into the water and then came forward in succession, a bottle of rich cream, a paper of sugar, choice ham, biscuits and cakes, which added to the several contributions of others to the party, soon manifested one of those ample preparations of food which in the open air by the running water are fed upon with a relish, peculiarly epicurean. We all fed sumptiously, finished with the coffee and the cakes and then after taking a drink from the clear creek, recovered our horses which had fed upon the young grass, and started onward for McKinney.*[181]

A camp at day's end with a group of kindred souls can be most agreeable, especially if those traveling members of the legal bar had just come back from Dallas where they had acquired a large bottle of German spirits and one of Kentucky whiskey:

> *Getting into Denton County, we passed over sparsely settled prairie for many miles until, toward the close of day, having lagged behind my companions, I saw before me, as I turned in a point of timber, a group of five persons in consultation near a clump of trees. One of them was enveloped in a red blanket and might easily have been taken for a party of half breed Indians. Nearing them, however, I found my own companions of the day. The District Attorney was the Knight of the Red Blanket. The subject of their deliberations was certainly a grave one, worthy of the learning, wit and eloquence which was drawn to its consideration. When we left Dallas in the morning, the kind hearted proprietor of the Trinity Exchange, who has animated regard for the comfort of the inner man, had suggested the propriety of taking with us a bottle of Krschen Wasser, which, if any of our readers are unaware of, I will certify that, while purporting to be some type of cordial, and looking very white and innocent like creme de cafe, will come as near burning a hole through the tongue or stomach as any other fluid I have ever tasted. The motion of our friend at the Exchange having been seconded and carried by a decided majority, the next difficulty was to balance the bottle which was very large and heavy, by a corresponding weight in other end of the saddle bag. Of course, nothing else but another bottle would do that, and as there was plenty of water on the route, it would have been useless to fill it with that and that milk, although a most meritorious drink would most certainly sour from being shaken. And at that moment it occurred to our considerate friend at the Exchange that the District Attorney was not adverse to the use of palatable fluids. No sooner thought than acted, a large champagne bottle was filled with Kentucky vintage and paced opposite the Krschen Wasser.*[182]

What to do with free time in town?

How did lawyers spend their evenings away from home? There was a wide range of activities, even a century and a half ago. Some were subdued - "lectures on phrenology", for instance. A visitor could attend "preaching at the courthouse", an activity Demorse thought demonstrated a commendable regard among the visiting attorneys for a proper observation of religious duties. Or he could listen to railroad proponents, trying to sell stock in proposed Texas rail ventures. Temperance speeches were also popular. DeMorse remarked wryly that in Dallas, on nights when these talks were given, "the decanters in the leading drinking house were dressed in crape."[183]

Some of the after work activities were pretty tame:

> *Dramatic Readings*
>
> *Miss Eloise Bridges entertained our citizens on Tuesday and Wednesday nights last with readings from various authors. The lady reads decidedly well - with dramatic effect and only needs scenery, dresses and foot lights to render her presentations in the highest degree effective.*
>
> *Her rendering of the balcony scene of Romeo and Juliet, the little ballad of Charles Machree and Hiawatha's childhood were excellent, though the comic passages from the play of the Dead Shot and from the Bedott Papers were most applauded.*
>
> *Her utterance, intonation, emphasis, gesture and posture are well conceived and executed with effectiveness. Very respectable audiences received her here and if she travels farther westward, we command her to the consideration of those who can appreciate something higher than Negro minstrels and buffoonery, We heard her but once but understand that on Wednesday night she had a good audience and gave much satisfaction.*[184]

School examinations in those days were open to the public and DeMorse attended some of them when in town, reporting back to his readers across North Texas. A music examination in Lamar given to the students of the Paris Seminary, for example, was declared to have drawn "a dense mass of visitors, filling the large room of the Seminary over full."[185] Ladies' Fairs, like the one in Lamar that raised several hundreds of dollars for the benefit of the Presbyterian Church, attracted the lawyers, who, according to DeMorse, were "among the young gentlemen who were willing to pay high for looking at pretty faces."[186]

At times, the lawyers found themselves in a town away from home on a holiday. For example, DeMorse celebrated Christmas/ New Year's of 1858/59 in Paris, Lamar County with "successive dances, explosions of Chinese Crackers, discharges of Anvillades etc."[187] They were in Hopkins County for the Fourth of July in 1850 and, with his colleagues partook of the hospitality of his friends there, "attending a 4th of July barbeque at the [Sulphur] Springs, 3 miles south of Tarrant and, we must say that we have not yet witnessed a public dinner of that kind conducted so well."[188]

The lawyers had their "days off", time to spend sightseeing and in day outings. Among the diversions on the road was fishing. DeMorse did not care for it, calling it "holding a line by the bank of a creek all day and catching more ticks than you do fish."[189] Nevertheless, the Judge and some of the other members of the team of traveling lawyers were avid anglers, even though, as DeMorse speculated that "between them all, they catch three or four little perch."[190]

> *At Bonham, we came upon His Honor, the Judge who was whiling away his time, in the interim between Hunt County and Collin, in luxuriously idling about fishing places, with the better part of creation. The Judge is a famous fisherman and can steadily hold his line in the water for hours without a nibble. In this most praiseworthy employment, His Honor was very ably assisted by a worthy member of the Bar from Lamar county, a gentleman of known gallantry, fascinating*

inner spirit and an elegant exterior."[191]

Despite such dispersions cast by DeMorse, fishing in North Texas was good. Clear Creek, for example, "abounds in fish which we have been enjoying for the past two days - perch, trout and buffalo plentiful."[192] After leaving Alton in Denton county "the Judge went to John Carter's below here on Clear creek to catch fish with a seine. At one haul last week, at a deep place, near Carter's, a thousand were brought out, an exercise which DeMorse said "much rejuvenated" His Honor."[193]

For those who did not fish, there were other ways to pass the time on the road. DeMorse describes a break in the travel and how some of the horsemen took advantage of it.

> *The district attorney is alternately discussing military marches upon a Meledeon and making himself interesting to the ladies; the legal gentleman from Denton is lying upon his back reading Ancient Mythology and your correspondent's occupation is indicated by this letter."*[194]

DeMorse wanted to observe this new country and sometimes he would persuade a host or local resident to show him around. In 1855, John Chisum, an early cattleman, brought DeMorse and some lawyers from Lamar and McKinney to a beautiful spot in Denton. DeMorse fell in love with it, fantasying that he some day would retire there - once the railroad was built, of course.

> *I have been riding about looking at the country, which is charming, and bathing in the deep clear basins in the creek. It is very luxurious to a gentleman who lives on black land where the streams have muddy beds to get up here by some clear basin in the creek, where the water is just deep enough and the bottom is firm and clean and there is a bank of sand at the margin of the water, to come upon and arrange one's toilet comfortably. I say it is very luxurious to enjoy the*

natural conveniences of the place and almost impossible to resist the impulse, as you see some choice little spot, apparently constructed, especially for a bath, to keep out of it, and as there is no necessity for keeping out, why, in you go, as a matter of course enjoy the luxury of laving in a pure stream and feel better after it and wish it was in your power to do this every day. After a while, when the Memphis and El Paso railroad runs near here, I intend to have a farm on Clear creek and come out frequently for fishing and bathing, fresh butter and rich milk. Antelopes and mustangs run about here now and tomorrow we go out to chase either or both.[195]

Court Week!!!!

Before sympathizing too much with the hardships which the traveling Texas lawyers of the 1840s and 1850s sometimes had to endure, consider that most every place they went a party was likely to break out.

When Court was in session, usually twice a year, for at least a two week period each time, the population of the town grew. It attracted a flock of lawyers, like DeMorse, from other counties, as well as the participants in the lawsuits - the plaintiffs and defendants, the witnesses, the judge, the jurors and the curious. Politicians, railroad promoters and pedlars of patent medicines and other products took advantage of the large crowds to ply their goods at the same time. During Court week in Grayson in 1859, DeMorse reported that "the Dental profession was well represented, there being no less than 5 practitioners from abroad, all present and operating on the people of Grayson."[196] Often, there was less painful entertainment during these court weeks: balls, horse races and traveling shows of different kinds.

Take Tarrant, in Hopkins County, for example. An eye opening report sent home by DeMorse about the colorful doings during Court week in April 1853 there provides us today with a flavor of both what constituted a good time a century and a half ago and the camaraderie displayed by this traveling troupe of lawyers.

First, there were horse races among the lawyers steeds. The field included the celebrated horse *Uncle Andy*, owned by Hon. Wm. H. Johnson of Titus; Frank H. Clark, Esq. of Red River's bay *General Cass*; Capt. John A. Summers of Red River's *Frosty*; B. W. Gray, Esq. of Titus's *The Dumpling Sorrel*; A. T. Howell Esq. of Red River's bald face pony *Choctaw,* and L.G. Harmon Esq. of Hopkins' *Bolivar.*

DeMorse described the entrants in Pulitzer Prize winning style:

> *The first race was between Uncle Andy and Frosty. To describe this rich scene would take a far more graphic pen than mine. The two horses were brought out for the admiration of the bystanders. Uncle Andy was a tall bare boned steed who had seen years and evidently experienced sorrow. His greatest fame had been in swimming creeks, which he rides over like a Leviathin. He had a neck like a fishing pole and a head like a churn.*
>
> *Frosty - the very remembrance of his "grave" appearance - makes my blood warm. As his groom brought him out and turned him once or twice to note his agility, his eyes fired up, his finger tail vibrated from right to left, like he felt the blood to his extreme and evidently the fire of a thousand contests had stirred his blood instantaneously, as the old familiar act of turning warmed his memory. Frosty had seen age as well as Uncle Andy, but was better preserved. He was compact and looked agile still and there was no appearance of grief or misfortune in his countenance.*[197]

Frosty was the crowd's favorite, and Johnson, *Uncle Andy's* owner, found many with whom to bet "recklessly hazarding his half dollars on his long tried companion." It took a while to find a rider for *Uncle Andy*. Betting was heavy and the two owners sat by the finish line. DeMorse takes up the action:

At last they came. For a while, there was little remarkable in the movement of either, but as the rider of Uncle Andy, forgetful of the proper dignity of his steed, ventured to strike him for the purposes of increasing his speed, the old horse indignantly commenced pitching and answered each blow with a vigorous kick. Shortly, outraged beyond endurance, he turned to a mound about halfway up the track, and refused to move further. Frosty, on the contrary, came through like an arrow and enriched his backers. Uncle Andy was withdrawn[198] *with serious complaints of hard usage and the honorable member from Titus, nothing discommitted and preserving only the recollection of his virtues, declaimed loudly about his swimming abilities.*[199]

After horse racing in the afternoon, the agenda each evening during Hopkins county Court week called for all night dancing to a hot fiddle. Widower DeMorse, who was there, tells about the night's fun and gives us today a glimpse of what a good time was back then. And it certainly does sound like a good time!

We have had more or less of the last night, every night, during the week and last night his Honor and a young MD of the vicinage, having made an excursion to the Sulphur Springs, returned with some interesting young ladies and we had the greatest fete of the week at our hotel last night. Dancing cannot be well done without music and music for a dance must have durability as well as vigor.

Tarrant is rich in musicians, old fashion fiddlers who play to amuse themselves all day, and then play the last part of the night for the gratification of others. Our main reliant is a character, one of those well contented fellows who would have suited admirably as a constituent of the early French villages of the best, without a care and leaving life to take care of itself. With a glazed cap set jauntily on one side of his head, and evidently all absorbed by contentment and melody, he played in the porch of the tavern, hour after hour, and then, at night, for the dance, without compensation. Such men are useful. They produce hilarity and contentment and a village without one is like a compass without a needle. Well, we danced last night! Every body danced; we had a responsible array of beauty; every body was gratified; nobody paid anything except of free will, for refreshments; we had glorious music, two violins and a tambourine, the last occasionally played on by sticks, as a drum, and, way after midnight, when I lay down in the room adjoining the dance, vigorously and merrily, in most excellent time, the violins were rendering their melody, the drum was beating in accompaniment, and my slumbers, light as an airy vision, were swept over by sweet strains, and that soothing tripping of the feet, which is certainly one of the most delightful sounds in the world, slightly softened.[200]

For those who did not dance the night away on the final night of Court week at Tarrant in 1853, there was other entertainment. A mock court, a Kangaroo Court, was sitting in the back room that playfully imposed punishments upon those adjudged guilty of the imagined offenses. Again, let participant DeMorse describe the proceedings:

All this time [during the dancing], another drama was carrying on in an adjacent room. A portion of the company whose love for the dance was surfeited by the entertainment of the previous nights, were holding high court and trying culprits for imaginary crimes, and decreeing and enforcing fines with a vengeance. The High Sheriff of the Country acted also as the sheriff of the court, and whenever it was necessary, arrested culprits with the assistance of a posse. The rule of evidence was that, if the witness failed to convict the accused, either by something he knew or imagined, or by something which somebody else might possibly know, for something the accused might possibly have done, whether he did it or not, he was himself substituted for the accused and a fine imposed. The Clerk, who was the Clerk of the District Court, certified the fines and issued execution, which was collected instantly, and Brandies, Cherries and cigars were plentiful in the court room. Nobody was exempt and nobody dared to resist. A plea to the jurisdiction was visited with summary infliction. We had a reach week of it.

Yours as ever,
C. De M.[201]

Dances on the last night of Court Week often lasted all night, with the next morning usually a travel day. DeMorse delighted reporting "the morning after" of a dance in Denton:

Friday night we concluded the services of court week with a dance, at which the grace and beauty of the vicinity presided until near day light of Saturday.

That morning, all our party being ready, we started for Gainesville, the county seat of Cooke county. One gentleman, who escorted a young lady to the dance at Alton and after dancing himself down and having gone to bed three times during the night, was waked up to escort her home in the morning and was perfectly astounded to hear her say that she was not the least tired and did want the dance to break up so soon, has recovered from his fatigue after sleeping on his horse halfway here and more than half the time since he has been here, and is now ready to test the activity and durability of the ladies of Cooke. The rest of the party are, as racing men would say "on their feet" and tomorrow rested, fed and recreated, we try the prairie of Cooke to take a look of the mustangs and the antelope.[202]

A grand ball in Porter's Bluff, once a thriving municipality on the Trinity River in County, which has since disappeared without a trace, drew the lawyers to a dance that lasted until 11 o'clock the next morning:

> *One object of our travel to Porter's Bluff was that there was to be a grand ball, assembling all the belles and the beaux of the country twenty miles around. As the evening advanced, in they came, in troops, and long before the night the violins commenced and the more ardent of the dancers opened the fete. The majority, however, reserved themselves till beauty should become more lustrous in the glare of concentrated light. After dark, the work commenced in earnest. About 50 ladies were present and a large number of gentlemen. I cannot say how many. The music was excellent and the prompting clear and in good time. Cotillions were the order of the night exclusively.*
>
> *In new counties, of all others, dancing is done with a zest and at the Bluff it was especially so. Until eleven o'clock, next morning, the sound of the violin never ceased for more than three minutes at a time. I went to bed about midnight but all night the violins sounded in my ears and, after breakfast in the morning, I went up to take a look at the dancers. The females all seem exhausted and they hopped through the measure of the dance, but the men, either through better power of endurance or because they had occasionally withdrawn end recruited their energies, trod the floor with undiminished vigor. After breakfast, however, the number began to decrease. In couples and in half dozens they mounted up and rode off home, some to go twenty miles after dancing all night.*[203]

They also attended a dinner and dance in Dallas that was part of a grand opening of large, new storehouse.

> *C. W. Adams & Co. have almost finished a large two story storehouse, in which on Friday of last week, before the counter and shelves were put in, a Grand Ball was given by the Proprietors, to which all the*

people in the country were invited. And they came in large numbers. It has been said that there were a 160 ladies present and gentlemen in proportion. It was an era for the Three Fork and I can tell that dancing parties are as well got up at the Forks as anywhere in Texas. I doubt not that the fete will prove a decided hit for the gentlemanly firm who gave it and who did not restrict themselves in furnishing room, music, but gave a splendid dinner that was set out in the upper story.[204]

If DeMorse had a favorite town in his two decades of crisscrossing Northern Texas, it was Jefferson. The people there were all friendly, and they loved parties with lots of eating, dancing and music. Visitors, like DeMorse, were invited right along:

The Town of Jefferson is lively in both business and pleasure. I was barely on the street on the morning after my arrival, when the first friend at whose store I had called pressed me into service for a "fish fry." His better half coming up directly after, determined the matter and gave to me and to several others our orders which were to repair to Stanley's warehouse on the Bayou and prepare to enjoy ourselves. Due preparation for this festivity had been made in little time for here those affairs are frequent and got up with much celerity. Stanley's warehouse is a large building constructed to be a cotton warehouse, but now used as a furniture depot situated at the margin of the water, with a large door at one end opening right on the water, which is perhaps 15 feet beneath. Some of that industrious class of hombres, who mistake patient labor for amusement, were seriously fishing when we arrived. Some ladies too were sweetening the toil by their presence. A goodly company was present by 10 a.m, and the time from then to about 4 p.m. constituted a day well spent, one of the most pleasant I have ever known for years. Two or three publically spirited ladies, and as many similarly inspired gents, superintended the preparations for the table, upon which, when the time of actual service was at hand, we found choice fish, bass, ham, tongue, cakes and champagne. But during the time that the few were working, the many were recreating. Sam Williams and Brother were there with violins and the dancing was spirited and luxurious. The glowing sunshine light could not penetrate the broad warehouse, which were darkened by the large space excluded from the sunlight and also by the trees around. The music by the margin of the water had, of course, an increased melodious, as everyone knows who has ever heard music softened by the contiguity of water. There were fast dances and then conversation spells, the communicants being broken into parties, dispersed about the large building. There was sometimes a song, with or without a banjo accompaniment. The party was entirely genial; everyone's face had a pleasant glow and I am sure that none that were present but will reckon the day with a white stone as one of the few deliciously spent. Mr. Stanley, the proprietor of the warehouse, getting short notice, had gone to work with all the force at his disposal and put out of the way as much of the stock of furniture, now much thinned out, and occasional sofas and chairs left in their places besides the walls, were of course eminently useful. Late in the afternoon, the party dispersed to prepare for the Ball at night under the immediate auspices of Old Sam.

At night, at the Albambra Hall, the beauty of the vicinity came together and a very pleasant time was had til near morning. Balls have occurred with frequency during the entire winter and I know of no place where the entire population is on better terms of pleasantness, each with the other than this. It shows what good might be done with a right start and the residence of a few genial persons, giving a right social turn to intercourse at the inception of a new place.[205]

It was not all dining and dinner, of course. Some of the towns, Jefferson included, also had professional entertainment during Court week. DeMorse was able only to see the end of the season but, a drama critic among all of his other roles, he panned the performance.

> *The population here has been regaled for the summer with something termed a theater. It has dwindled down of last to one stick of a fellow, who advertised a general performance, in which all the parts of Macbeth and William Tell were to be performed by himself - not read, but acted. I went last night and beheld a personage with distinguished legs and a visage like a Prairie Bull, which, whether he appeared as male or female, hero, woman or sailor, never changed but had the same unalterable expression of the prototype through the most comic tragedy or tragic comedy.*[206]

Chapter Eight

Sight seeing and discoveries along the way

Customarily - although not always - county seats were roughly sixty miles distant from one another. This was the distance that DeMorse and his party had to ride between court appearances. The farther west they went, the more frontier it became.

Texas was still new - at least to the eyes of the white man - and often wild, when DeMorse and his cohorts at the Bar crossed it. There were wonders to behold and DeMorse, like any tourist, took some snapshots of what he and the others had witnessed in their travels.

Take wild life, for example. The eastern edge of the North Texas prairie abounded in game in the 1850s, but even by then, the buffalo there were already disappearing, although yet numerous elsewhere on the continent. DeMorse reported in *The Standard* on a visit to Fort Worth in 1853, when it was still a military outpost. It gives today's Texan a glimpse of days gone by.

> *At [Fort] Worth, we found in the line of curiosities, a wild cat, a pet bear, and an immense pair of deer's antlers, picked up on the Grand Prairie, probably 4 feet in length. Wild animals brought up the subject of buffalos and we learned that, a few days before, a party of soldiers coming from [Fort] Belknap to Worth had seen a solitary monarch of the prairie wending his way to the Cross Timbers. None had been seen in the vicinity for long before. The Indians have nearly exterminated them from the Great Plains but, nearer home, in an uninhabited swampy region between Chambers Creek and the Trinity, there is a herd of a hundred or more, which have never left the old pasturage, but out of the ordinary course of travel and seldom seen, still remain a memento of the native*

populations of the broad green plains, over which the encroachment of the white man brings civilization, but destroys romance.[207]

The band of traveling lawyers sometimes encountered large herds of antelope as they traveled from county seat to county seat. For example, DeMorse describes the antelope and their habitat he encountered en route to Gainesville in Cooke county:

> *On Sunday morning last, I left the capital of Cooke and wended my way westward. From the crossing of Elm Creek, near Gainesville to Clear Creek, we rode over a fine body of prairie, crossing several creeks and branches, whose borders were covered by timber. We saw a herd of beautiful antelope, ten in number, on a high point of prairie near Wadsworth's Bluff, a romantic and picturesque eminence, rising abruptly from the edge of a lovely and retired looking valley, to an elevation of some hundred feet, behind which the broad and undulating surface of the fertile prairie extends for miles. It is a favorite feeding haunt of the antelopes.*
>
> *They seem to be ever on the watch. We had not approached closer than a mile, when they elevated their heads, moved restless about and gazed at us apparently sniffing the "tainted gale." Then, as we gradually neared them, they trotted to and fro arranging themselves in a line, fronting us, and, on nearer approach, suddenly wheeled into a line and, in perfect order, bounded away over the slope of a neighboring ridge. I could not then but wish for a fresh steed and a brace of greyhounds to chase the antelope over the Plains. But the sun was shining hot and my good steed somewhat jaded, so I continued my wonted pace of a slow walk.*[208]

Wise County, which "abounds in antelopes", was on the edge of the frontier in the late 1850s. Demorse had an opportunity, while visiting Sweet Water, the home of Col. Land's, Wise's representative to the legislature, to observe two young, recently captured antelopes at play.

> *"There were two young ones in the yard caught shortly before by running them down. Their horns were not grown and, consequently, they did not have the goat appearance which they maintain when mature. Delicate looking creatures, they were prettier than fawns, with finer heads, the ears long tapering and generally bending inwards at the extremities. The eyes were very large beautiful and protruding so that they can almost see behind them. The eyeball could easily be destroyed with a side shot without injuring the surrounding skin. The color is similar to the fawn, rather lighter with white sides. Around the tail which is a short tuft the hair for several inches circumference is white and when they run the tail is thrown up. This white hair is all erected and has a beautiful feathery appearance. In running, they do not leap like the deer but run level like a horse, except that it is much more rapid. These little things, if petted a while, will follow one around the yard and occasionally canter about very prettily. They are beautiful pets and domesticate in an hour or two.*[209] *Whether they would become troublesome like a deer when larger, no one here knows. When grown they become heavier than the deer. They have been seen in groups near deer and, when started by dogs at the same time, far outran the deer. They are seldom killed and, when killed, in hilly terrain from covert. They are good food. When run by dogs or otherwise, they cannot be driven to timber but will keep high points on the prairie, and if necessary they will pass close to the pursuers in order to keep in the open prairie.*[210]

Panthers were also found in Northern Texas during the 1840s and 1850s. Judge Evert, who was traveling by himself, ran into one almost face to face near the East Fork of the Trinity, an animal which "he took to be a tiger and which, it being peaceably disposed"[211], he carefully avoided. DeMorse allowed is was "the second "varmint" seen in our travels. One of our company saw a wild cat in the tree on the way from Greenville to Bonham, in Bois D'Arc bottom.[212] On another occasion, DeMorse had the opportunity to see one close up and preserved the picture for us today:

> "*We stayed at Bonham there one day and observed the remains of a large animal killed near town which we were requested to examine and identify. The skin had been stuffed and placed in the upper room of Mr. Doss' store. Going there, we found what I was first disposed to call a cougar, but which others believed to be a panther. Having seen no menagerie for years, I yield the point. It had a round short head with dangerous looking tusks, was six feet long exclusive of the tail which was two and a half feet in length. The color was that of a deer in the summer. It measured when killed 15 inches around the arm. It was a really fierce looking personage, but like most wild animals, ran when discovered, and being pursued by dogs, took a tree. While in the tree, it was shot. Having just finished a repast upon pork, it was probably disabled from active defense.*
>
> *While on the subject I might mention, living four or five miles from Clarksville, James Clark killed four panthers near his residence a few days since.*[213]

Deer can still be found in North Texas, although not in herds the size that DeMorse and his companions observed one afternoon, while taking a short cut in Collin county.

> *Getting to the Hackleberrry Tavern [near Millwood, Collin county], we concluded to take a course across the prairie instead of following the road. By this course, we saw herds of deer in such numbers as it was common to encounter them in Texas a few years since. They were grazing by the banks of the little prairie branches where they were usually undisturbed*

by the approach of travelers. Shortly after leaving the road, we started about 30 in a herd, then we came upon about 14, then upon 31, next 27. As we approached them, they would draw together to concert their movements, then watch us for awhile, and at last as we got near them, they ran fleetly from us. The last gang divided. Some took down the branch, others crossed over and giving notice to a party on the far side of the timber which fringed the banks, they all scampered off together, occasionally turning to take a look at us. As the sun went down, a bright moon shown upon us, and spreading out upon the prairie and riding rather briskly, rather after the style of a steeple chase, we had a delightful and refreshing ride.[214]

Wild turkeys are distinctly American. The Pilgrims had them for the first Thanksgiving and they greeted the pioneers as they went west. The band of lawyers riding the circuit observed them on the frontier of Johnson, Ellis and Tarrant counties. DeMorse relates one such encounter, while on their way to court in Dallas.

On our way, we started a wild turkey from her nest under a bush and then arose a nice discussion between the Court and the District Attorney about the feasibility and desirability of picking off the eggs. Both seemed to be agreed as to the removal of the eggs, until they began to consider whether it could be safely done. About the time the court considered that they may get mashed in the saddle bags, a more liberal idea struck him that it might be better to leave them to be hatched where they were and to someday have the sport of shooting the product. The District Attorney who thought they might make a nice accompaniment to "a gentle drink" of some generous fluid, was not able to understand the philosophical forecast of his Honor in its full extent, but compromised by leaving the greater portion of the eggs to be changed into turkeys for the benefit of the sportsmen, some day hereafter and taking only three or four in his hat.[215]

There were other fowls besides turkeys to attract the attention of the lawyers. In Hopkins county, for example, they observed "prairie fowls, literally in the thousands, [that] made the air vocal."[216] These huge flocks of pigeons and their natural choreography captured the attention of a visitor to DeMorse's band of traveling lawyers. His reaction - and DeMorse's description of it - gives us a glimpse of Nature's mastery:

> *There was a continual flight of wild pigeons, before, above and behind us. During the passage of the last two miles between Robbin's and Becknell's prairie, the sight was really novel and wonderful. They kept a continuing whirring like the sound of a rapidly approaching storm. They moved above us and before us in dense masses. Occasionally, they gyrated in the shape of a water spout upon the ocean and settled for an instant in the woods, then rose again and flew a short distance and repeated the descent. As we emerged from the timber upon the prairie, having on our right a body of timber reaching down to the roadside a short distance, their continued movements across the point of prairie, their various evolutions, curving, recurving, embodying in dense mass, then running out into a long line, were very beautiful. It was in the evening and all tended to be moving northward, toward their roost in the Pine woods, where they hold their winter occupancy. A friend from New Orleans who was with us and, to whom the sight was new and intensely interesting, could not cease his exclamations of admiration, as long as they were in sight, but kept turning back and calling on us to notice each new and beautiful evolution.*[217]

It was not just animals that got DeMorse's attention. He was deeply interested in botany. He had his own vegetable garden and fruit orchard and experimented with a variety of ornamental trees, shrubs and flowers at his home in Clarksville. In fact, he is credited with having introduced the chrysantium to

Texas, having brought some bulbs back from a trip to Philadelphia. Texas offered many exotic wild flowers and DeMorse was in his glory in his travels, as the four following of items from *The Standard* illustrate.

> *On the way, we found some prairie flowers which neither I, nor my companion, had ever seen before. They were at the edge of a hollow, on rocky land, and were clusters of small bells upon an upright stalk, four or five inches high, of a magnificent deep pink hue, resembling most in general appearance and effect, thought somewhat different in conformation, the deep pink hyacinth with single bells, thickly clustered about the stem. They were indeed superb. Digging around some of them with my knife, I got a long slim hard root, in shape like a carrot, and cutting off the tips, will endeavor to get them home alive.*[218]

> *The writer left Buchanan, day before yesterday, after dinner. Three miles of prairie and we entered the Cross Timbers, through which our course for several miles. Getting out of this belt, we came once more upon the prairie, rich and covered with myriads of gorgeously rich flowers there were thistles of different species and the richest colors and shades that I have ever seen. There was the royal purple, the deep reddish purple, several shades of pink and deep pink and purples with lighter shades in their centers and some with white centers. Some were globular in the center some were flat or nearly so, with a rich fringe looking like French pinks, except infinitely richer. There were not merely clusters of them; there were endless millions, in some places standing over hundreds of acres like the stems in a wheat field. In all these in a travel of several miles, I saw only two with white blooms, the rest were all colored.*[219]

> *Yesterday, I visited the Valley of the Brazos. Cactus, the Standing Cypress and a variety of prairie*

flowers, that I cannot identify, were before us immediately upon crossing. The Cypress or Texas Plume has been frequent ever since we got into Parker County, not growing as in garden culture, six or eight inches high, but between two and four feet and shaking in the breeze, from the tall stems a more gorgeous flaming red plume of florets thickly clustered around two to four inches of the top of the stem.[220]

Our route from Denton Creek to Decatur had been mostly over high prairie, with many poor rocky and clayey points. One of these poor points was profusely covered with flowers, in the greatest variety of colors richly blended. I have never before seen such quantities so crowded together and learn that they were never seen in such quantity prior to this Spring. At almost every point, the cactus is intermingled with the flowers, mostly the common prickly pear, but with varieties of shade, the prevailing color being yellow. Many of the cactus were every double in flower and looked almost like roses.[221]

Besides flowers, DeMorse and friends encountered ripe Chickasaw Plums one "of excellent flavor, growing on bushes some six feet high"[222], wild onions, "plentiful and of good size"[223] and wild grapes suitable for wine making:

We came to abrupt elevations, termed in the field notes of the survey of the upper Brazos region, "Mountain Bluffs." They were steep rocky elevations, the sides of which were sometimes perpendicular and showing at times solid ledges of rock, broken into occasional gorges, filled with wild grape vines, while the bold sides of the hill were covered with Juniper. Beach grapes, or rather grape vines of they have no fruit on them this spring, had bushy looking vines, not more than two three feet in high, but with smooth leaves but having the usual shape of the grape leaf and the tendrils of the vine. These I was informed bore usually a most delicious grape, small and of a dark color. The grapes in the mountain are a sort of Fox grape, an excellent choice for wine. They bear profusely. It struck me that right here, where they grow naturally, protected from severe cold by these mountains ridges, vineyards may be successfully cultivated. The soil and situation do suit.[224]

There was even a curiosity of a tree that caught DeMorse's eye.

Just a little before getting here [Weatherford], on a little prairie drain, we saw a conjunct tree, by the roadside which was a curiosity. Before getting close to it, it was evident that coming out of the center of a stately spreading elm, came up as the center and topmost part of the tree, a Hackleberry shoot. The contrast in foliage in color was striking. When we got to it, we examined it. The tree was a cluster of five distinct prongs at the ground which presented a united top. One of these shoots from the ground was the hackleberry, which grew up distinctly, perhaps six feet tall, then inward to the center of the tree, between two prongs of the Elm, had united on each side with the elm and palpably grown together so that the three parts had become one and then the Hackleberry pushed straight up through the center of all the branches and presented this strange evidence of a double tree of two species. If there were not an absolute junction of the woody fiber, at least the union was such that nothing but a cutting off of the entire bark, could have detected any division. The bark itself across the three prongs presented an indivisible surface.[225]

The minerals of North Texas too were interesting - and potentially valuable - discoveries for the riders. Indeed, on one occasion, DeMorse was pleased to see that his horse had eaten so well at the ranch of a host as it needed strength "to pack geological specimens, cactus etc in addition memorandum books and clothing."[226] He was not exaggerating if the following report was typical of what he collected on a trip.

> *Coal - Yesterday, I went out in company to visit some high peaks visible at the left, immediately in crossing the West Fork, after coming from Decatur, to this point. Four of these as I came along the road seemed to be formed in a circle, as though artificially cut, but getting to them I found their forms irregular. The ascent was quite precipitous but we got up them on horseback. The sides were thickly covered with rocks which lay about the edges of the top. The general surface was level with some soil upon it and some grass, flowers and cactus growing upon it.*
>
> *Before ascending the ridge we went in a ravine for specimens of coal. Cropping out the sides of the ravine was lignite, not much advanced beyond the stage of charcoal. Some looked fairly like charcoal, some like bituminous and some was mixed with sulphur of iron. My saddle bags are too heavily laden to allow me to bring in large specimens. Petrified wood, very fine specimens, were lying about. At another place that I have not been able to visit lies a bed of perfect coal, semi bituminous and harder than this I have, but in use it has not proved valuable, running too much to cinders.*[227]

DeMorse and his comrades at the Bar also discovered some interesting, but long dead, plant and animal life - fossils.

> *Stopped before night at this place, the residence of Mr. Dickson who has lived here for about 4 years. Found here, some petrifactions, one a piece of wood that had been split with the grain by a knife, rather light of weight but emitting a fire when struck with a knife blade. Another, having the appearance of a coffee mill handle, with the hole through it the iron, looking like heavy dark sandstone; another a petrified terrapin with all the creases of the shell still distinct. Plenty of*

ammonites are found here. The rock around here is a conglomerate of clay and sand, easily pecked by a knife but enduring fire and atmospheric action. At Dallas, Mons. Gonhenault showed me the petrified bark of a tree four inches through. The inner wood was gone, but the bark was perfect, with pebbles adhering to it. The piece of tree I have was found in the open prairie.[228]

Have today been on the hills by the bottom and sauntering about for curiosities have found upon the summit scallop, oyster and mussel shells petrified. The oysters were most of them in halves and at first I was disposed to doubt their identity but at last I came upon one whole, whose rough coat and irregular shape could not well be mistaken and, putting the point of a big knife to the seam, it opened so familiarly that I almost expected to see the ancient inhabitant within it.[229]

Flora, fauna and fossils were not the only exotic life that DeMorse and his companions happened upon during their travels. He encountered some honest to goodness frontiersmen as well. The following accounts tell of some of them:

A mile and a half from Sister Grove, upon a high prairie point adjoining the bottom, we came to the place of Mr. Walden, a frontiersman by birth and habit, the son of the first white settler above St. Louis. He had been stockaded from the Sacs and Foxes during his entire boyhood and so debarred an education. Moving from western Missouri to Texas a few years since, he has kept upon the outer edges of the settlements most of the time. Though, now within them, his location is an isolated one with all the peculiarities of the frontier.

He has only one neighbor who lives four miles off. Around him are unsettled bottoms and in getting from his house, as in getting to it, our path was through a narrow pass through a thicket impenetrable to anything but bears or small varmints, except by the trail he had cut out. The prairies, hemmed in by the creeks, and constituting this isolated domain, were very fine high rolling and very rich. Over these the mustangs still rove as they did in earlier days over the whole region and our host had been endeavoring during the day to shoot two leaders of a gang, which he was afraid might lead off some of his own horses. My readers out of Texas might not understand that domestic horses sometimes get in with the mustangs and are afterwards as difficult to secure as the mustangs themselves. Two large bear skins stretched out to dry and sundry deer horns about the fence, the Bee trees, cut off and moved to his house, the deer skin hunting shirt of the proprietor and his cap of the skin of a wild cat, denoted plainly enough that we had intruded upon the domain of a hunter.[230]

Passing over the rich prairie of Dallas, with the lofty term the Mountain looming up on the other side of the River all the time in view, after traveling 15 miles, we got to the Ferry and crossed without difficulty, and by about sundown, got to Frank Jordan's 15 miles east of Birdville. Frank Jordan was not home that night. He got home the next night after swimming a creek as usual. Frank is a well known personage on these frontiers, who trades about generally, contracts with the garrisons for supplies, never stops for high water and can swim a river on horseback driving a yoke of oxen in before him, and leading two ponies in the rear without any sort of trouble. As he is really an extraordinary man, not in talk but in fact, I must account a bear killing of his that goes far beyond Gen. Putnam's wolf killing, which, by the way, as much as the biographies make of it, was really no great feat. About a year since, when Frank was sheriff and, on his way home to where court was held, somewhere on the Grand Prairie near Fort Worth, he overtook a large sized bear, some distance from timber and immediately determined on attacking him. He had no weapon with him and first commenced by charging up to the Bruin on his pony and beating him over the head wit one of his stirrups. This broke without having hurt the bear. Frank then took out his pocket knife which had one large blade and then charged up and cut his antagonist with it. On the second time he attempted this, Bruin snapped at his hand and took out the inside of his cuff of his coat. For some time he continued this, wounding and worrying the bear and keeping him away from the timber and in the course of the fight running him about 12 miles. Frank's blood was getting warm and his want of success in seriously disabling the bear roused his determination. Dismounting and gathering up an arm full of buffalo bones, he broke them over the bear without producing any effect. He then tried another plan and determined to attack him on foot with his knife. Accordingly, seizing the Bruin first by one hind leg and then the other and pulling off as the bear would turn around and snap at him, he finally succeeded in cutting off his hamstrings and thus getting him off his feet he dispatched him with repeated thrusts without much more difficulty. As soon as the excitement of the contest was over, the victor found himself sore in every part of his body. He is a powerful tall rawboned man, but the exertion had been tremendous and the muscles of his arm were black as though bruised by a serious blow. Of course, the bear was wearied in the long chase and to some degree affected by the repeated cuts with the knife, although small, but it was such a fight as few men would have followed to the end. The bear was subsequently seen by several persons and Frank's account of the fight sufficiently proven, besides the fact that he is known as a man of veracity.[231]

The prairie we passed over was very rich and very pleasantly undulating and our traveled terminated at sundown at the place of Mr. Brown, in the Northwest corner of Ellis county, a pleasant little nook at the edge of Post Oak timber and near a small creek. The situation was very pleasant and reminded me of the peasant homes in humble life which we read of in books, but find so seldom in our travels. Mr. Brown is an old frontier man, a perfect specimen, in fact, rough but simple, cordial and genial. He was born in Tennessee, raised to manhood in Kentucky, lived in Illinois and Missouri and fives years ago, he came to Texas and settled at his present residence. Then there was no one near him except two gentlemen by the name of Myers, still living neat the little village of Alvarado, not far distant. There was but one room and a shed to the house. For occupants there was the old man, his wife and two sons, young men, each with a wife and yet our company of three and a distant neighbor who was cow hunting, were all made comfortable, fed well, and had good beds.[232]

The Caddos, who inhabited parts of North Texas, had a tradition of mound building. Could the mounds in the following piece be of that type?

Six or seven miles this side of Spring Creek saw a mound in the prairie upon which were two piles of rock; went up and examined the place but saw nothing more of than a pilot monument for the original Indian occupants of the region. The settler, who was traveling with me from Spring Lake, told me that in the neighborhood there was one mound with the same appearance.[233]

The political entity of Texas was not very old when DeMorse and the other members of the Bar traveled it. Yet, it already had a history, one deeply respected by DeMorse, as evidenced by his reports on visits to historical sites.

At about 19 miles from Dallas, we crossed the Elm Fork of the Trinity River, at the ford where General Tarrant crossed with the men from Red River and Bowie, in the Indian Expedition of 1840, when Denton was killed.

Passing through Elm bottom our attention was called to a large tree by the roadside, from which a square of the bark had been cut, and on the inner surface of which someone had delineated with a pencil in large fair Roman letters: "Cherokee Exploring Expedition, September 1845." The letters were still plain, although the bark had begun growing over the beginning letter "C." [234]

In an 1853 visit to Tarrant county, DeMorse, in an effort to preserve history, sought out the site of Bird's Fort, abandoned some dozen years earlier. Micahah Goodwin, one of the first settlers, was his guide. DeMorse's description of approaching from the east, that is, from North Dallas, provides us with an idea of the geography we now associate with the Dallas/ Fort Worth Airport. To avoid fording the swollen Elm Fork of the Trinity at Dallas, DeMorse and his party had traveled north, some 15 miles, on the Dallas side of the river before crossing it. Then he headed west, across the Grape Vine Prairie to a settler's home, where he spent the night. Next day, he pressed on, passing streams, like Bear Creek and Fossil Creek, more familiar today to Dallas Metroplex golfers for courses that carry those names, than to historians.

The reader of 1853, as well as the one today, learns from DeMorse's report on the trip, something of the history of the founding and abandonment of the Fort, information that otherwise might have been lost to posterity.

It had been the first settlement made in Tarrant County in 1841. It was a daring enterprise of the little band who had pushed out to the Indian country, hauling all their supplies from Bonham. Bird took with him into the wilderness 19 families, including twenty five men. They built several houses and enclosed three of them with a stockade. In January, 1843, they were ordered off by the agent of the Peter's Colony and were thus broken up. One of the company was killed by an Indian, while cutting a road through the timber.

Anxious to see all the noted localities historically connected with the first settlement of the country before every vestige of their primitive face is erased by the hand of improvement, about a mile from the River, on a level prairie, we came upon the margin of a lake in the shape of a crescent, about 300 yards wide in the center and coming to a point on either end. Within the area, enclosed by the semicircular water, a high point of land puts it probably 15 feet higher than the surrounding prairie. This land was originally all timbered, but close upon the lake the timber had all been cut down by Bird's men, probably as a matter of protection as well as utility, and the land had been put to cultivation. Upon this, a young growth had sprung up. None of the structure of the fortification remain now. No land is in cultivation yet and the place looks much as though no one had been there to change the aspect that time has given it, since the first pioneers had left it. Fire from the burning of the grass has erased the houses and the picketing that had enclosed them, but we could trace the places where they stood and the line of enclosure which was near the center of the point, close upon the water. Bird is dead, died in Titus County in peaceful territory and the place would now, years after its settlement, still repose in lonely beauty.[235]

The same year, 1841, as the establishment of Bird's Fort saw another important settlement in Tarrant by M.T. Johnson at Mary Le Bone Springs. It came to be known as Johnson's Station, three miles north of present Arlington. DeMorse visited there as well and, en route, passed another significant spot in Texas history, Tarrant county's in particular, the site of the Battle of Village Creek. It was here where General Tarrant led the Rangers against the Indians and where preacher/soldier John Denton was slain. DeMorse described what the Indian village looked like. He regretted the passing of the Indian life in the face of the advance of "manifest destiny." Yet, he respected Denton and even planned to recover his body for reburial:

Five miles before getting to Colonel Johnson's, we came upon the beautiful valley of Village Creek, the scene of the fight in which Denton was killed in 1841. The only traces of its former occupancy now remaining are the broken ground where the Indians tilled and at the foot of the mound overlooking the field, a circular plot of ground very carefully prepared, as level as a floor, with an embankment about it 18 inches high, which is suppose to have been their dancing ground. The frames of the wigwams have long since disappeared from the burning of the grasses. The creek is a clear running pretty stream with gravelly bed. Every time I see an Indian village I am compelled to admire their taste in the selection of a home. Almost always by a clear running stream, with the field in a valley of sandy loam and a hill or high point of country overlooking it all, they seemed intuitively to combine the useful and the beautiful, and it is not strange that recollections of boyhood linger fondly about such scenes and that with a sunken reluctance, yielding only to superior force and manifest destiny, they give place to the encroaching footsteps of the palefaces. My readers will recollect that it was a force from Red River (our home) which under the command of General Tarrant that drove off these marauders upon the frontier. The village was made up of an amalgamation of Cherokees, Caddos, Wakoes, keechlea, Ionies, Anadarkos, Tawacannos and Muscagos, in all 150 lodges. Col. Denton who has been depicted in some romantic tales as the Warrior Preacher of Texas, was the only man killed and he was slain in the creek by some Indians in ambuscade, before the body of the men came up. His body was carried by his men some 15 miles and buried in a creek bottom and so covered as to conceal it from Indian observations. Those who buried it have never been back to look for it, but [its location is estimated] from their account of the course and the distance that the grave is by the creek. Last Spring as we went up to Denton county we discussed a project for hunting the grave and disinterring the bones of the warrior Preacher but our information was too indefinite to act upon. My own opinion is that Col. James Bourland, whose knowledge of courses in the wild country is remarkable is probably the only man who could find the spot. He thinks that by commencing at the battle ground he could from his recollection trail the place and find the grave, having some remembrances of surrounding objects. [236]

DeMorse also visited another honored spot of Texas history - a large double oak tree, the site of an 1842 treaty with the Indians. He thought it would be preserved forever. Has it?

There is nothing remarkable about Mr. Johnson's locality for a residence. There is something, however, in the history of the place. Immediately before the house is a large double oak, under which the treaty of 1842 with the assembled Indian tribes was made by General Tarrant and Terrel and John Durst as commissioners, under the immediate supervision of President Houston, who was present. From a projecting limb waved the flag of the Lone Star and the historical incident will probably perpetuate the tree. It has been mostly shorn of its limb this spring in an effort to re-invigorate it.[237]

DeMorse even got a glimpse of the future - the age of machinery ushered in by the Industrial revolution which was making its way to Texas.

As we got near Bonham we took the right fork of the road and visited William's Mill, the wonder of enterprise. It was Sunday but we found Mr. Williams at home and he guided us through the mill, then at rest. First we looked at the machinery. The boiler is 40 feet long and was hauled on an immense wagon of 6 broad wheels constructed for the purpose, hauled by numerous yokes of ox and occupied several months in transit from Houston. We next carefully examined the Engine, a specimen of machinery that quickly brought to mind the machinery on first class Northern Steamers, with its fine finish, all bright as a new dollar, its governor, cut off valves, and every possible attachment calculated to make it efficient for the best service.[238]

Chapter Nine

The War Between The States

As the year 1860 began, an era in Texas was about to end. It had been a busy quarter century since Texas had earned her independence from Mexico. After a decade as an independent Republic, she had joined the Union of American States, becoming the 28th State of the United States.

Then, trouble in paradise. For complex reasons, the Southern and Northern halves of the nation became at odds on a number of issues, not the least of which were the institution of slavery in the South, the call in the North for it abolition and the rise of the Republican party. Many in the South were grumbling what would happen if the "Black Republican", Abraham Lincoln, was elected in the November 1860 election.

In June 1860, even though the breakup of the Union was but six months away, there was no sign of animosity in *The Standard* as DeMorse encouraged the citizens to prepare for the upcoming July Fourth.

> *Eighty four years ago the independence of the United States was declared. On that day a nation was born, destined to outvie any of antiquity in the form of government, the dispensation of its laws and the fruits of its resources. Everywhere is felt the power of these United States, the strength of its institutions and the stability of its government. Over every quarter of the globe floats the star spangled banner waves and the American citizens in foreign lands are beneath its folds, conscious of its protection. Throughout the Union, in every little village and hamlet in every state, the influence of the day will be felt. For one day at least internal dissension and political wrangling should be forgotten and all unite in celebrating our nation's birthday.*[239]

But with the election of Lincoln in November, there was no ignoring the problem. Over in Lamar, the future was the subject of a "mass meeting held in the Baptist church which was filled to overflowing." A committee of twenty one had been appointed the week before and eight of them signed the "minority report" which began:

> *Whereas, for the last 30 years, there has been gradually organizing in the North, a great sectional party, whose sole object is the abolition of slavery in the southern states; and*
>
> *Whereas, the recent election in the United States for President and Vice President has resulted in the election of Lincoln and Hamlin, the candidates for those offices proposed by the abolition party; and*
>
> *Whereas, we the citizens of Lamar county regard said election as a clear and unerring indication of public sentiment at the North in reference to our constitutions and;*
>
> *Whereas, the first law of nature is self preservation*
>
> *RESOLVED*
>
> *First, that we regard the election of Abraham Lincoln and Hannibal Hamlin as a declaration of hostility on the part of the North against the institutions of the South and so regarding their principles; we are in favor of resisting by the best and most effective means which can be adopted by the states to be injured.*
>
> *Second, to form a convention of Southern States to negotiate and reach a compromise with the Free states.*
>
> *Third, that we regard the so called "Personal Liberty Bills" which most of the Northern States have enacted as a direct nullification of the Fugitive Slave Laws and the Constitution and such an outrageous aggression upon our rights as cannot and will not be tolerated; that we are in favor of requiring of our*

northern brethren an unconditional repeal of these obnoxious acts, also our just and equal rights in the common territories of the United States and in short to all the rights to which we are entitled under a strict and literal interpretation of the Constitution. Should they agree with these, we will remain in the union and support and cherish it as heretofore; but should they refuse these guarantees, then, in our judgment we should form a separate Confederacy of such states as will unite in the movement.[240]

Texas lawyers were in the thick of it. Attorneys F. W. Miner, N. W. Townes and B. H. Epperson were among those who signed the minority opinion. Judge H.S. Bennet and lawyers George W. Wright, W. J. Bonner and W.B. Wright were in the majority.

As 1861 began, however, the minority in many places became the majority - and very quickly like a wild fire. Northern born DeMorse was among those changing position week by week:

It is too late now to form patchwork treaties. The Union is dissolved. Today there is no United States of North America as was lately known. So the Union cannot be saved because is "non est"[241] *and may be reconstructed and hope it will be. It is said to be like a wall you had to go the base and reconstruct that and it is mere charlatanism to talk now of tinkering with then pieces that have fallen out.*[242]

Less than a month later, DeMorse became even more resigned as to what lay ahead.

Many of the truest and wisest patriots hoped and believe that a firm presentment of Southern demands, within the Union, would elicit a just response from the North. But there is no room for hope now unless we first go out and defiantly set forth our demands, not with bravado but with unmistakable determination, that, already out, we will not return. The day of compromise has passed. Those who want unity must come to us. We ask no privileges, only the little right of equality and to be let alone.

There is no other feasible way now. To recede from this would be futile. We had as well write "Fool" across our skull caps and take seats which would render it convenient to spit upon us.

We hope the Union will reconstruct. We believe it will. The time has come for the Right to command and not to beg.[243]

Finally, two weeks later, DeMorse accepted reality. The was no more Union among the states and he favored Texas' secession:

Everyone who reads the Standard knows that we are no extremist or disunionist. We have not given up hope that the glories and benefits of the Union are to be perpetuated. Yet, so hoping, we shall give this day our vote "For Secession."[244]

Increasingly the call came for a convention to determine what course of action the state should take. South Carolina had already seceded by December 1860 and state secession conventions were scheduled for Mississippi, Florida, Alabama, Georgia, and Louisiana in early January. After some struggle with Governor Houston, the convention in Texas was held but its choice had to be ratified by the people. DeMorse reported the results of the election. It was far from unanimous in Northern Texas:

The Election

Red River gave a majority of 63 for secession; Lamar 81 against. Fannin we understand has given something under 200 majority against secession. Grayson is said to have given near 500 majority against secession. In Harrison county the vote stood for secession 866 against secession 44. In Cass and

Marion we are told it was almost all for secession
Hunt gave 74 vote majority for secession
Bowie was 268 in favor and 15 against.[245]

Symbolically to mark the change, DeMorse redesigned *The Standard's* masthead adding the Lone Star with the legend "a Democratic Republican Journal." DeMorse explained his reasoning for the change:

> *The State of Texas having resumed her Sovereignty, the act being complete, there can be no proprietary in the continuance of the Standard of the late Union at our editorial head. We therefore make a change conforming to the change of circumstances, by which as a citizen of Texas, we are now necessarily and willingly governed.*[246]

As would be true with all Texas institutions, the law courts were affected by the upcoming hostilities. For a while, the lawyers seemed to act as usual. News reports on the courts indicated that some lawyers kept at it as long as possible: Wm. H. Johnson and J. W. Miner from Lamar; B. W. Gray, Josh Stevens and Malcolm Bolin from Titus; Martin Hart from Hunt, W. T.G. Weaver from Cooke; Binkley and Hendricks from Grayson, W.B. Wright and J. A. N. Murray of Red River all practiced to the end.[247]

But, by year's end, the Courts were beginning to shut down:

> *The members of the Bar at Houston requested Judge Palmer to continue the civil docket to the next term in course. Recognizing their right to control their own business, he did this.*
>
> *If witnesses can be procured the criminal docket ought to be cleared. Justice to accused persons and justice to the community demands this. Also where parties are ready in litigated civil matters - titles to land etc. - the dockets should be cleared of them. It is*

important as a moral issue that the courts of the country should not be closed to demands for personal protection, to the protection of the equilibrium of social organization and the punishment of depredators.[248]

The editor of this paper was in Lamar county last week. Not much was done with the civil business the citizens having requested that no judgments should be rendered in civil cases and to equalize the matter with all parties the magistrates were requested to take no action and promptly consented to the suggestion. The criminal docket was set over to Monday of this week. What has been done on that we do not know. The only attorney present from another county, except the district attorney, was J. A. N. Murray Esq. of Red River county.[249]

The editor of this paper was in Bonham court last week. Judge Waddill opened court on Wednesday evening and pushed the business through to completion, probably adjourning on Monday of this week. No time was lost in idle dalliance at the expense of the county. Judgments were rendered on civil suits until the receipt of the Stay Law prevented further action in that line.[250]

There was a call for soldiers and the North Texas counties provided many to the Confederacy, Red River among them. Soldiers were sworn in with the public watching, with newly appointed Judge R. L. Waddill doing the honors and DeMorse reporting it:

It was a rather impressive ceremonial, when the town magistrate administered the oath to support the Confederate states, to the successive platoons with hands upraised, Judge Waddill then by request addressed the company from the platform of the Courthouse, alluding the cause in which they had volunteered to serve and the motto of their flag -

Our rights or death

The men responded with three cheers for Jeff. Davis and the Southern Confederacy, three cheers for Beauregard and three cheers for Judge Waddill. [251]

DeMorse's son Leslie, a member of a newly organized Red River County, wrote his father from Bonham on May 8, 1861, a classic "*When Johnny Goes marching off, hurrah, hurrah*" letter.

Dear Standard:

Notwithstanding the disordered state in which we left Clarksville, all arrived safe at camp 1 and ½ miles south west of Paris on the same day we left. Early we proceeded to organize, electing officers which resulted as follows:

Jas. E. Hopkins - Captain

Thomas R. Wilson - First Lieutenant

John L. Hart - Second Lieutenant

John C. Burks - Orderly Sergeant

Jas. H. Clark - Assistant Sergeant

Les C. DeMorse - First Corporal

W. P. West - Second Corporal

John Ward - Third Corporal

John Gordon - Fourth Corporal

Jasper A. Barry - Surgeon

John T. Montgomery - Assistant Surgeon

Wm. Guest - Ensign Bearer

At every place we have entered our flag has been welcomed with loud huzzas and the waving of handkerchiefs by the ladies. Along the road we are greeted repeated with "Hurrah for the South" and "Long Live the Red River Volunteers" and, in some instances, the ladies were weeping. This demonstrates the spirit of enthusiasm that is prevalent among the masses. With such shouts of cheer as these which serve to nerve and cheer us, and armed with the right, can we fail to conquer?

Red River county mustered into service about 140 men all told.

Les[252]

A number of the lawyers from North Texas, who had written the circuit with DeMorse, joined on the side of the confederacy. Samuel Bell Maxey was a natural. A West Point graduate[253], he had fought in the Mexican War. After secession he resigned his position as district attorney for Lamar county and formed a company called the Lamar Rifles. Later he received permission to form a regiment, the Ninth Texas Infantry. He was promoted to brigadier general in March 1862 and subsequently, on December 27, 1863, was appointed commander of Indian Territory, where he served until February 21, 1865[254]

John Jay Good of Dallas organized a confederate artillery battery. Wounded in battle, he was then appointed presiding judge of the Confederate military courts of Mississippi, Alabama, and Georgia, with rank of colonel.[255]

Judge Burford, resigned his post to join, as a private, the First Texas Artillery under Captain Good., a former law partner of his. He received a commission in 1862 as colonel and raised a regiment from Dallas, Kaufman, Ellis, Hill, Navarro, McLennan, and Parker counties. [256] Cyrus K. Holman was part of Whitfield's Legion, the First Texas Legion and the Twenty-seventh Texas Cavalry, which was one of the two first legions that Texas provided to the Confederate States Army.[257] B.F. Farney became a lieutenant of the Lamar calvary.[258] Later, he enrolled a regiment of infantry for Brig. Gen. Ben

McCullough.[259] Judge Ochiltree, was elected to the Provisional Congress of the Confederate States but resigned to return to Texas and raise a regiment.[260]

DeMorse himself was to leave the newspaper and go off to war. In 1862, he organized and became colonel of the Twenty-ninth Texas Cavalry, which saw service in Indian Territory and Arkansas. It bore the brunt of the fight at Elk Creek or Honey Springs in 1863. He also commanded the Confederate forces at Poison Springs, near Camden, Arkansas. They halted an attempted federal advance into Texas from Little Rock.

Not all fought as soldiers. Tol Guest could not because of an injury suffered just months before in an expedition against the Indians. Others helped out in their own ways. For example, *The Standard* noted that "Geo W. Wright from Lamar, was in town Monday on his way south east to procure arms for his country. He was furnished $2,000 from our county treasury for a similar purpose."[261] J. A. N. Murray and Geo. Bagby each subscribed twenty five and fifty bales of cotton to the cause.[262] John Crockett, of Dallas, resigned as lieutenant governor of Texas to become superintendent of the Confederate arms factory at Lancaster. N. C. Gould, another lawyer, became the enrolling officer for Red River county which was expected to provide a hundred men.[263]

A company from Red River expressed its thanks for this help from the loyal public.

> *We are requested by them to return their thanks for assistance in outfit to W. F. T. Hart for provisions; Capt. Henry Little for bridle, saddle, blanket, money for one man. E W. Gaffeney for horse an pair of navy six shooters; L.H. Norwood for a horse and Chas. DeMorse for short sword and rifle.*[264]

> *On Thursday evening six more young men made an independent start from this vicinage for*

McCullough's camp. These are Leslie DeMorse, Powhattan Ware, Sam Anderson, John Marti, Wm. Duke and Louis Igo. They were well mounted and armed and seek service. This little squad return their thanks to John S. Gordon & Son for pack mule, Dr. U. H. Ware for pack horse for pack horse, Dr. J. Bagby for pistol; H.R. Latimer for shot gun; W.L. Nunnely for pistol; Cap't Rich'd Giddens for $15 cash; J. N. B. Donoho cash advances; N.C. Gould for saddle and Dr. T. P. DeVere for lots of medicines and prescriptions.[265]

Some of his comrades on the legal circuit who had gone off to fight kept DeMorse posted. For example, Wm. C. Young wrote:

> *By yesterday's mail I received orders to raise 1000 men, to be composed of companies of infantry from the counties of Bowie, Red River Titus, Lamar, Hopkins, Fannin, Hunt, Grayson, Collin, Cooke and Denton for the protection of the northen border of our state. The troop to furnish their own arms etc., to be called for one year unless sooner discharged. I hope the countries will respond immediately with companies of 83 or even 100 men. The emergency requires primeness and dispatch.*
>
> *Companies raised under this call will report to me at Gainesville, Cooke county immediately.*[266]

Attorney Jim Farr reported that "at a large and enthusiastic meeting of the citizens of Hunt, irrespective of party, the following resolution was unanimously passed: Resolved that we do pledge our property, our lives and our sacred honor to sustain the Confederate States in the present crisis for right and reason. We have considerable war spirit among us."[267] W. B. Sims, another lawyer, wrote DeMorse and told how he and others had marched to the Indian nation where "we have this day planted the Confederate flag upon the enemy's soil, and there is not one in the regiment but will not die in its defense."[268] He added: "I start an express tomorrow morning to Fort Smith for more ammunition and as many arms as we could get. Give us good arms and warm clothing and we bid defiance to the enemies of our country and the chilling winds of the north. The boys area all in fine spirits and prepared and willing to go into battle at any time."[269]

George H. Bagby enlisted in the Confederate Army but was discharged from active duty because of his older age. He later served as paymaster and traveled in 1863 Arkansas to pay the Texas troops. On the return trip through Indian Territory, he was attacked and killed by Indians.[270]

A "Home Guard" was formed in most towns to protect against any enemy invasion. M.L. Simms commanded one Red River unit and William Stout another at Blossom Prairie:

> *On Saturday last this company turned out in full uniform. After having marched around the Square the company proceeded to the Methodist Church for the purposes of receiving a flag presented by the fair sex, the execution of which reflects credit upon those engaged in the work.*
>
> *Miss Belle Gordon on behalf of the Ladies in an eloquent, well delivered and appropriate address presented the Flag. M.L. Simms Esq in his usual felicitous style responded on behalf of the Company,*
>
> *On Monday this week the Company again drilled, much to the satisfaction of all present, evincing some skill in acquainting themselves with a tact totally novel to most of the members.*
>
> *We desire to see this company prosper and are satisfied that under the present energetic and efficient commanding officer, it will. We are glad to see the dormant patriotism of the people of Red River county has at last been awaken Military companies have been*

organized, we under stand in every precinct in the county. This is as it should be, whether in time of peace or war, but at the present time, decidedly opportune.[271]

They have a company at Blossom prairie of some sixty odd men and at Garvin's about the same. We meet every Saturday for drill.

W.B. Stout [272]

Not all of the North Texas bar were in favor of secession, yet only one joined "the other side." Judge Everts was a Unionist and opposed secession. He moved Navarro County and spent the war quietly there, returning to the Bench after the end of hostilities. B. H. Epperson, also was a strong opponent of secession, but after secession, he came to support the Confederacy. He ran unsuccessfully for the Confederate Congress in the fall of 1861. Lameness in one leg kept prevented his fighting , but he contributed money and supplies to the war effort.[273] William H. Johnson was a delegate from Lamar County to the Secession Convention in Austin and voted against leaving the Union. He later was lieutenant colonel of the 22nd Texas Cavalry regiment which was made up almost entirely with former Unionists.

The exception, Martin D. Hart of Hunt county, played both sides and earned the reward for such treachery. While Hart had originally opposed the movement, he seeming was converted to the Texas cause. In July 1861, he organized and led the Greenville Guards, a company of mounted volunteers. He pledged the company's services "in defense of Texas whenever she is invaded or threatened with invasion."[274] In the summer of 1862 he received a Confederate commission with permission to raise a company and operate in northwest Arkansas. This got him through the Confederate lines, where he and his men surrendered and joined the Union cause. Hart led a series of attacks upon Confederate forces and was said to have murdered two secessionists. Captured by the

Confederates, he was court marshaled and hanged on January 23, 1863.[275]

As dastardly as Hart's behavior was, it was balanced by acts of patriotism and heroism as that of young John C. Burks, a young Red River lawyer and frequent companion of DeMorse in riding the circuit. He helped raise a company and captained a company that became part of Col. William C. Young's Eleventh Texas Cavalry. Later, he commanded the regiment.

He went off to war in a flourish:

I learn that two more counties have been called for from Red River. This will certainly drain the county of men who can go for war." I now lay down my pen to grasp the sword

I must as the official of the company bid our friends a parting farewell - for the many kindnesses to the company I return warm thanks. If we meet no more it will be a consolation for them to know that we died in defense of home and liberty

John C Burks [276]

In May , 1861, he reported on the Red River Volunteers' encampment at Honey Grove in Fannin county.

We camped four miles this side of Paris last night and organized this morning before taking up our line of march.

We are well and in fine spirits. We have heard many rumors but nothing definite, more than you know

In great haste

Jno C. Burks

P.S. We will camp 8 miles west of here tonight. We have about 100 men and a s good looking a

company as ever paraded on the battle filed.
I shall write you again.[277]

On December 31, 1862, Burks was slain while leading a charge on a Union battery at Murfreesboro, Tennessee. According to reports, while "holding his hand on the wound to control the bleeding, he continued at the head of his command, urging his men forward, until he lost consciousness. In his report of the battle, Gen. Mathew D. Ector said of Burks: 'a better friend, a warmer heart, a more gallant leader than he was, never drew the breath of life.'"[278]

Burks was not the only one not to come back. DeMorses's son Leslie died returning home after the war.

APPENDIX

Professional Cards

Anderson county

Craven & Good

John Craven & John Good

Palestine, Anderson county

will give prompt attention to all business entrusted to them in the District and Supreme Court of this state and in the United States Courts for the District of Texas

references: Scott & Holmes of Palestine and S. H. Morgan Esq. and Summers & Clark of Clarksville

Bowie county

E. H. Tarrant & S.M. Peters, Attorneys at Law, Boston, Bowie County, Texas

will attend all the District Courts in the Eastern portion of the Republic and the Supreme Court.

S. H. Pirkey , B.T. Estes, Wm. M. Campbell

Pirkey, Estes & Campbell

Boston, Bowie

will practice their profession in the 8th Judicial District, Bowie, Cass, Titus, Hopkins, Hunt, Fannin, Lamar and Red River; also in the Supreme Court and in the Federal Court in Tyler

R. M. Lindsay Attorney at Law

Boston, Bowie

any business tended to him will be attended to promptly, will practice in all the counties of the 8th Judicial District, to wit Lamar, Red River, Bowie, Cass, Titus, Hopkins, Hunt and Fannin counties and in

Harrison county in the Sixth

Cass and Marion counties

Theodore Cameron, Attorney at Law

Jefferson, Texas

will practice in the 6th and 8th Judicial Districts; also in the Supreme and Federal Court at Tyler

Collin

A. H. Martin

McKinney

will practice in the District Courts of Dallas, Collin, Denton, Grayson, Ellis and Tarrant

Thomas Lewellen

McKinney

J. H. Harberger, Attorney and Counselor at Law

will practice in the District Courts of the 8th Judicial District and promises that "undivided attention will be given" and that "particular attention to the collection of claims and the prompt remittances of funds collected. He will also act as agent for the purchase and sale of lands."

John C. Easton, Attorney at Law

McKinney

will make collections and attend to land claims in Collin, Dallas, Ellis, Tarrant, Denton, Cass and Grayson counties [Cooke, Johnson and Parker counties were added to and Cass removedfrom the list in 1861]

Cooke county

W. T. G Weaver was the District Attorney of Cooke county

according to accounts in *The Standard.*

Denton county

An attorney named Mr. Carroll was identified as an attorney in Denton according to accounts in *The Standard.*

Dallas county

John J. Good, Attorney at Law

Dallas

practices regularly in the District Court of Collin, Grayson Denton, Tarrant, Parker, Johnson, Ellis, Dallas and Kaufman counties and at the Supreme Court of the state;

particular attention given to land titles and collections

"He has long resided in this portion of the State and flatters himself that the liberal patronage heretofore extended to him is a sufficient guarantee of his ability and prompt attention to business."

Office on south side of Main street in the building formerly occupied as Clerk's office

Burford & Dyer

references: J. W. Smith & Co in Dallas; A.M. & C. C. Alexander in Dallas; A. Caruth & Brother - Dallas; Shepherd & Gordon, Nashville, Tenn.; J .R. Anderson of Nashville, Tenn.; Alexander Allison of Nashville, Tenn.; Turner, Williams & Co. of New Orleans

Crockett & Good

will practice law in the courts of Collin, Kaufman, Ellis, Tarrant, and Dallas counties and in the Supreme Court of the state at Tyler

special attention will be given to handle taxes, soldiers claims and claims against the State

B. Warren Stone

Dallas

will practice in Hunt, Collin, Denton, Kaufman, Grayson, Ellis, Tarrant and Dallas

An attorney named Mr. Nicholson was identified as an attorney in Dallas according to accounts in *The Standard.*

Fannin

G. A. Everts

Bonham

will practice in the counties of the 8th Judicial District, Kaufman in the 9th and in the Federal Court at Tyler

R.H. Lane

Bonham

will go to Fannin, Grayson, Collin, Hunt, Hopkins, Lamar, Red River and Kaufman

William M. Woods, Attorney at Law

Bonham, Fannin County

will practice his profession in the counties of Northern Texas and will pay particular and prompt attention to the collection of all claims entrusted to him

Turner L. Green, Attorney at Law

Bonham

has removed to Bonham and will in future devote himself to his profession

Stanford T. Burney, Attorney at Law

Bonham

will practice in the 8th judicial district, also in the Choctaw and Chickasaw Nations; will also secure business licences for those who want to trade with the Nations

T.F. Smith, Attorney and Counselor at Law

Burleson, Fannin County

will attend to any legal business entrusted to his care

Other attorneys named Samuel A. Roberts, a Mr. Davis, a Mr. Howell, a Mr. DeLisle, a Mr. Collane, Robert H. Taylor and Col. Land were identified as an attorneys in Fannin according to accounts in *The Standard.*

Grayson

Williams, Milwee & Townes

offices in Sherman, Grayson county and Paris in Lamar

will practice in the 8th judicial district and in the Supreme court

C. C. Brinkley, Attorney at Law

Sherman, Grayson county

attends to business in the counties of northern Texas, especially Grayson, Fannin, Cooke, Denton, Collin and Wise

Burrill P. Smith

Sherman, Grayson county

Other attorneys named Mr. Hendricks and Mr. Marshall were identified as attorneys in Graysons according to accounts in *The Standard.*

Hopkins county

H. C. Russell

Tarrant

will practice in all the counties of the 8th Judicial District

Malcolm Bolin

Tarrant

references from Washington DC, Mobile and Montgomery Alabama, Austin and Jefferson

E. D. McKenney, Attorney at Law

Tarrant, Hopkins county

L. E. H. Houghton, Attorney and Counselor at Law

Tarrant, Hopkins county

E. J. W. Tomlinson, Attorney at Law

Sulphur Springs, Hopkins County

will attend promptly to all business entrusted to him

Address: Bright Star, Hopkins county

W. M. M. Ewing, Attorney and Counselor at Law

Tarrant, Hopkins county

will practice in Lamar, Red River, Hopkins, Hunt, and Titus counties; will attend to the collection of all claims entrusted to him and to all notarial business

S.S. Weaver, Attorney and Counselor

Tarrant, Hopkins county

Hunt county

A. T. Howell

Greenville

will practice in the several courts of the 8th judicial district

J. M. Leach, Attorney at Law

Greenville, Hunt county

will practice in all the surrounding counties. All business entrusted to his care shall have prompt attention

Jim Farr, Attorney at Law

Greenville, Hunt will practice in the District court of Hunt and the surrounding counties; also in the Supreme and federal Courts in Tyler

Kaufman county

Edgeworth and English, Attorneys at law

Kaufman Texas

will practice in the courts of the 9th Judicial district and attend to the land and collecting business in Northern Texas generally

Strict attention given to perfecting and quieting titles to land

Jim G. Thomas, Attorney at Law and General Land Agent

Rockwall, Kaufman county

will practice in the counties of Hunt, Collin, Grayson, Cooke, Montague, Wise, Denton, Kaufman and will attend promptly to the collection of claims and all business entrusted to his care.

Lamar county

Cyrus K. Holdman

Office in Paris, Lamar

perfecting land tittles and the collection of debts in Northern and Eastern Texas

J. N. Guest, Attorney at Law

will practice in the courts of the 8th judicial district, comprising the counties of Lamar, Red River, Bowie, Cass, Titus, Hunt and Fannin

address: Paris, Texas

R. Peterson, Attorney at Law

Prairie Mound, Lamar County

Ben F. Farney, Attorney at Law

Paris, Lamar

will practice law in Lamar, Red River, Bowie, Cass, Titus, Hopkins, Hunt and Fannin counties comprising the 8th Judicial District and in the Supreme Court of the State and the United States District Court at Tyler

Office on the south west side of the Public Square

W. B. Wright, Attorney at Law

Paris, Lamar

will practice law in Lamar, Red River, Bowie, Cass, Titus, Hopkins, Hunt and Fannin counties, comprising the 8th Judicial District, and in the Supreme Court of the State and the United States District Court at Tyler

Rice Maxey and S.B. Maxey

R. and S.B. Maxey, Attorneys at Law

Paris

will practice in Lamar, Red River, Hopkins, Hunt, Grayson and Fannin counties; investigate land titles; pay taxes for non residents and attend to the collection of debts in any part of Texas

S.B. Maxey is Commissioner of Deeds for the states of Virginia Kentucky, Tennessee, Alabama, Arkansas and Missouri

W. H. Johnson, W. M. Williams, N. W. Townes

Johnson, Williams & Townes, Attorneys at Law

Paris, Lamar

will practice in the 8th Judicial districts and the Supreme and Federal Court at Tyler

Red River county

Charles DeMorse, Attorney and Counselor at Law,

Clarksville

will practice only in Criminal Cases and the collection of Foreign Debts.

Hervey Dillahunty

has settled in Clarksville and will attend the court in Red River and adjoining counties and the Supreme Court at Tyler

office on the Public Square, next door to W. P. Dickson & Co.

Summers & Clark

Jno. Summers and Frank Clark

"collection and settlement of claims from a distance; letters requesting information in regard to Texas lands, title etc, when accompanied with a fee, will receive prompt attention."

office next door the District Clerk's

Clark also separately advertised himself as a commissioner of deeds nine states, New York, Pennsylvania and California among them, "for the acknowledgment of deeds, mortgages etc."

N.C. Gould , Attorney and Counselor at Law

Clarksville

will practice in all the Courts of the 8th Judicial; District and Supreme Court of Texas

U.S. Commissioner & Notary Public

Clarksville

Office upstairs in the Courthouse

John A. Corley, Attorney at Law

Clarksville

has removed his office to the east side of the Public Square and will continue to practice in all the county of the 8th Judicial District

Jas. H. Clark, Attorney & Counselor at Law

Clarksville

Office next to store of John Gordon

Sutton & Sutton

Red River county

Courtes B. Sutton in Clarksville

Norbonne E. Sutton in Kiamitia, Tex

will practice law in all the courts of the 8th Judicial District and in the Supreme Court of the State

George F. Conly, Attorney and Counselor at Law

Clarksville

B. H. Epperson and M. L. Sims

Epperson & Sims, Attorneys at Law

Clarksville

office: second door, west of Russell's store

John C. Burks, Attorney at Law

Clarksville

will practice in the 8th Judicial districts; also in the Supreme and Federal Court at Tyler

special attention given to collection of claims, investigation of land titles, writing deeds &c.

Hervey Dillahunty and C.B. Sutton

partnership in Clarksville

office: first door south of Norwood's corner

Wm. E. Wootten, Attorney at Law

Clarksville

particular attention will be given to the collection and securing of claims

references include Rev J. W. P. McKenzie, president of McKenzie Institute and Wm. M. Harrison & Co. of Clarksville

Judges, Hon. J. B. Wootten and Hon. L. G Childers were identified as from Red River county according to accounts in *The Standard.*

Titus county

William H. Johnson, Attorney and General Land Agent

Mt. Pleasant

perfecting land titles, procuring patents to land, paying taxes upon land, redeeming lands sold for taxes, buying and selling lands etc.

Mills & Moore

Mt. Pleasant District Courts of the Red River district, also Cass county, the Supreme court of the state and the Federal courts of the State at Galveston and Tyler

Byrd W. Gray

Mt. Pleasant, Titus

will practice in Hopkins, Rusk, Upshur and Red River counties and in the 8th Judicial districts and the Supreme and Federal Court at Tyler

B. W. Gray and E. D. M'Kenney

Gray at Mt. Pleasant in Titus county

E. D. M' Kenney from Tarrant, Hopkins

will practice law in all the courts of the 8th Judicial District and in the Supreme and Federal Courts at Tyler

Malcolm Bolin, Attorney at Law

Mount Pleasant, Titus county

Commissioner for Alabama and Notary Public

Other attorneys named Mr. Hill, T. J. Rogers, and Joshua Stephens were identified as attorneys in Titus according to accounts in *The Standard.*

Travis County

S.T. Newton, Attorney and Counselor at Law

Austin

will give particular attention to the land laws and practice the investigation of titles to lands and all professional business entrusted to his care

Raymond Freeman and Co., Attorney

real and personal estate brokers, general Collecting and Land agents -

Austin

Upshur county

Martin Rogers, Mr. Camp and Mr. Galloway were identified as attorneys in Upshur county according to accounts in *The Standard.*

Wood county

A Mr. Sparks was identified as an attorney in Wood county according to accounts in *The Standard.*

ENDNOTES

1. *Going to Court in Texas* is seen through the eyes of Charles Demorse, attorney and newspaperman. A bit about DeMorse might better aid the visualization of the scenes he depicts. A 1941 volume entitled *Charles DeMorse, Pioneer Editor and Statesman*, by Ernest Wallace, is a complete biography of this journalist. It is based, in part, on information from DeMorse's granddaughter, Isabella DeMorse Latimer, as well as from an article DeMorse himself wrote in the *Standard* in 1872 about the early days. See also, Sheppard, *An Editor's View of Early Texas* (1998).

DeMorse was not Texas-born. Nor was that his real name. Most came to Texas from a far different lifestyle elsewhere in the world. DeMorse was no exception.

Born in Leicester, Massachusetts, on January 31, 1816, he was christened Charles Denny Morse, the middle name being his mother's maiden name. His forebears on both sides had been English settlers who, in the 1600s, had sought religious freedom in New England.

DeMorse's early years were in Leicester, where Charles' father was an innkeeper. It was a community in transition from agriculture to cotton manufacturing. Mills, full of immigrants spun into cloth that unique fiber called cotton, shipped up from the plantations of the South.

Charles Morse's mother was to die at the age of 29. Widower Morse, his sister, also widowed, and young Charles moved to New Haven, Connecticut, where again the elder Morse operated an inn. Some years later, they moved a third time, to New York City. Here, Morse ran the well-known colonial era Tontine Coffee House at the foot of Wall Street, then, as now, the heart of the nation's financial market.

It was in New York that Charles began to "clerk" for the New York law firm of Inglis and Van Wyck. Van Wyck, Morse's mentor at the firm, had a brother-in-law, also a lawyer, named Samuel Maverick who had just gone to Texas and fight in the

Revolution against Mexico. Young Morse had a hankering for something different from that of the practice of law, even if it were in the *de facto* capital of America. Inspired by Maverick's letters home, Morse joined a brigade of volunteers ready to sail for Texas and glory.

En route, their vessel, the Brig *Watawomkeag* was taken by a British warship whose captain thought the Americans were pirates. After a month in jail, they were tried in Nassau and acquitted. During Morse's detention there, however, a British officer made a clerical error that "re christened" him Charles DeMorse rather than Charles D. Morse. Viewing the error as a mystical merger of his long-dead mother's maiden name, "Denny", with the paternal "Morse.", he immediately began using this new name exclusively. He later had it changed legally to "DeMorse."

Reaching New Orleans, after some more adventures, DeMorse and the other new recruits traveled by land from there to the war front. En route, they met the captain of the schooner *Independence*, one of several vessels which comprised the new Republic's Navy. He signed DeMorse up as a first lieutenant of marines. DeMorse almost got to fight in this famous Battle of San Jacinto. Hurrying to the front, he was close enough to hear the booming of the cannons before the battle ended in victory for the Texans. Mirabeau Lamar, a Texas hero during the Revolution and later a President of the Republic, was to become a close friend of DeMorse. Later DeMorse was to exchange his commission in the navy to become a major in the Texas army, a title he would retain for the next two decades, until becoming a colonel in the Confederacy.

The army disbanded with peace, DeMorse resumed the practice of law, not in New York but in Matagorda, Texas, at the mouth of the Colorado River as it emptied into the Gulf of Mexico. Settled ten years before by fifty two families from New York and New England, it already, by 1832, had 1,650 inhabitants.

DeMorse was six feet tall and lanky, which reportedly made him look even taller. He had a large forehead, extended by beginning baldness, giving the impression that he had a brain larger than others. A short brown square-cut moustache was his only facial hair, and he was meticulous in his dress and habits: linen suits, with black string ties, in summer; dark and conservative suits in the winter. He was well-mannered, did not smoke and apparently drank rarely. He was not a churchgoer, but was certainly a believer in the Deity.

It was in Matagorda that DeMorse married Lodiska C. Woolridge, a well educated woman from Alabama and Mississippi, whose father was the American Consul to Matagorda. Together, Charles and Lodiska would have five children, four of whom would live past infancy.

DeMorse's Wall Street experience, together with some of the contacts he had made during the war, paid off. President Lamar appointed as a "stock commissioner", responsible for refunding the Republic's national debt, incurred in its War for Independence.

DeMorse had a third job as well - reporter for the *Daily Bulletin* in Austin, which focused on the Legislature. This experience exposed DeMorse to the smell of printer's ink, which became his permanent addiction.

Clarksville was the thriving seat of the giant Red River District of North Texas, parent to thirty nine present day Texas counties. Its merchants and town leaders wanted a newspaper. Some of them knew DeMorse, having been in a party with him that guarded the captured Santa Anna after the Battle of San Jacinto. The members of Congress of the Republic of Texas who hailed from the Red River District knew him also. A delegation approached DeMorse and asked him to set up shop in Clarksville. He did and nearly fifty years of *The Standard* were the progeny.

Thus, at the age of twenty six. Being in Texas some six years, Major DeMorse, his wife and their newborn son, Leslie Cazneau DeMorse, traveled the 500 miles from Austin to Clarksville in the spring of 1841. There he bought an old log cabin to house his press. He also bought a double log house for his family.

For most of the coming years, DeMorse would edit *The Standard*, the most influential newspaper in Northeast Texas and, for many years, second in circulation for the entire state, with agents as distant as Philadelphia, New York and Boston.

But twice a year, usually in the spring and the fall, DeMorse would turn over the paper to an editor *pro tem* and he would team up with some other members of the Texas bar, - a judge, a prosecuting attorney, and both plaintiff and defendant counsel - and together, on horse back, criss cross Northern Texas, trying cases in towns still being born. It is Charles DeMorse, the lawyer, who most interests us.

2. In the United States, the legal systems of nearly all the states are adversarial in nature and based on the common law inherited from England and its Anglo Saxon forebears. Some states, however, like Louisiana, Florida and California, which had been colonized by the French or Spanish, followed the "Roman Law" of their homelands, a non adversarial system which traced its roots to the Justinian Code in 534 A.D. Texas, although colonized by Spain and then Mexico, seems to share little with the Roman law.

3. These District courts and counties under their jurisdiction should not be confused with the sixteen Judicial Counties established by the Texas legislature, beginning with Trinity County, on February 5, 1840. They were all abolished by a Texas Supreme Court decision, *Stockton v. Montgomery* (1842)

4. That Judge was also to serve on the Supreme Court of the Republic. In 1845, just before Texas joined the Union, this second duty of the District Judges was eliminated.

5. It was not until 1876 that an intermediate level of appellate courts - the Court of Appeals - was established.

6. For the non-lawyer, the difference between "law" and "equity" depends upon the type of relief requested. Claims for money damages, such as for personal injury or breach of contract, fall on the "law side", while requests for a divorce or an injunction are on the "equity side."

7. Texas, as a Republic, was comprised of twenty three municipal districts, most of which had already been set up by the Spanish and Mexican governments. Soon, those districts were reduced to counties. The Red River District today is all or part of thirty nine counties.

8. The county judge, called "chief justice" initially, was appointed by the Congress of the Republic for four year terms. The office was made elective in 1841 and its term of office shortened. Later, its name was changed to county judge, and the term was again four years. The office was abolished in 1869 but was re-established in 1876. The main duties of the county judge are varied. He presides over the county commissioners' court, oversees the budget and elections and is a judge of the county court.

9. including today's Morris and Franklin counties

10. including today's Rains and Delta Counties

11. In 1856, the busy 8th Judicial District had a part of its circuit placed in the 16th Judicial District.

12. March 29, 1856

13. Due to a fear during Reconstruction that Southern that state courts would not vigorously enforce federal law, federal courts were given authority to decide "federal questions", that is, lawsuits arising under federal law.

14. In 1879, the Northern District was established and, in 1902, the Southern District.

15 November 29, 1856

16. Mount Vernon, Lamar county, was first settled in the late 1830s and early 1840s, and in June 1843 the county seat was moved there from Lafayette and a log courthouse was constructed. The next year the county seat was transferred to Paris.

17. See generally Welch, *The Texas Courthouse Revisited.* Reportedly, T. J. Shannon, with a team of six oxen, dragged a tree through the brush and briars to clear a road to Sherman. Id. at 91

18. A jacket would be hung from the tree into the pockets of which mail would be left to be taken by the next person heading to a more traditional post office. Id. at 91

19. Visitors would hang their saddle bags, with their valuables, on the trees branches, when they went into town. According to local legend, there was never a violation of that trust. Id. at 91

20. The logs, sometimes whole and sometimes planked with ax and adze, were laid horizontally and notched together at the corners. The chinks between the logs were stopped up and plastered to produce a tight wall. A one log room was usually about sixteen feet square, with an exterior chimney and front and rear doors to aid ventilation. Sometimes, two log rooms were joined by a breeze way and covered with a common roof. Their height was usually only a single-story.

21. November 21, 1857

22. July 3, 1858

23. March 3, 1855

24. November 29, 1856

25. See *Courthouses of Texas, A Guide* by Kelley ,and Dyal at p.79. See also *The Texas Courthouse Revisited* at 49

26. July 24, 1851

27. Eight years later, DeMorse again recollected the days of the old court house and, not unlike many of us when we go back in time, the memory varied a little. The old court house was even smaller than his first recollection of it:

> *Gainesville I find much improved. Though still a village, it looked more town like than six years since, the courthouse and one resident comprised the town and the courthouse was a log cabin ten feet by twelve feet in diameter, the space between the logs open, without a door with two rough benches and the Clerk's office kept in the Clerk's hat. The same grey haired gentleman is still clerk but he has now more official conveniences. The Courthouse is not much to boast of but it is a material advance upon the first edition which represented the corporate dignity of the county.* May 29, 1858

28. November 27, 1852

29. This structure served until 1878 when it was replaced by a two story brick building that cost over $25,000 and which burned in 1909. A fourth court house with 60 rooms and electricity was built in 1911 at a cost of $150,0000.

30. May 12, 1855

31. July 2, 1853

32. July 2, 1853

33. See *Courthouses of Texas,* by Kelley , and Dyal at p.14. See also Welch, *The Texas Courthouse Revisited* at p.91

34. May 8, 1858

35. October 9, 1852

36. June 28, 1858

37. May 19, 1847. A decade later, in December 12, 1857, DeMorse complimented a renovation that had just been completed on the court house: "The Court room has been plastered and furnished with comfortable sets and is much

improved in appearance". It would stand until 1873.

38. February 28, 1852

39. It would not be the last. Impressed by the brick, which was made locally, other citizens would soon use it in their own new constructions, including DeMorse who built a new building for *The Standard* out of brick.

40. August 14, 1852

41. September 30, 1852. DeMorse may have been pleased with the Clarksville courthouse in 1852 but, by 1858, he was finding some faults with it too. He thought that it should have been larger, "at least 50 by 75 feet." He also thought there was too much wasted space on the first floor, the offices "far too small" and that the shape of the roof gave the courthouse an "unprepossessing appearance". He concluded, however, that "the Clarksville courthouse is better than any other near it, but it is far from being architecturally in good taste or conveniently divided within the first story." May 8, 1858

42. The Texas Courthouse Revisited at 91.The present court house was built in 1935 at a cost of $306,000.

43. November 1, 1856

44. November 21, 1857

45. The April 16, 1859 issue contained a notice to bid.

BIDS W ANTED

Sealed proposals will be received through the third Monday in May next, for building complete a brick court house (say 50 by 60 feet and two stories high) for the county of Bowie; plans and specifications can be seen at the office of the county clerk of Bowie county at Boston:

W.E. Estes,	*C.M. Wassil;*
John A. Talbot;	*S. H. Pirkey:*
A.G. Haskins	*Building Committee*

The contract terms are not far unlike construction contracts of today: "Sealed proposal for a new courthouse for

Fannin brick or stone 60 feet square; payments to be made: $2,000 when the materials for the walls are delivered on the ground prepared for putting up; $1000 to be paid when the walls are put up to the second floor and the joist laid; $1000 to be paid when the walls are completed and the upper joists laid; the balance of the contract will be paid when house enclosed (half) and when work completed (second half). "May 14, 1859

46. "The editor of this paper attended Grayson Court during the first week. The new courthouse was occupied by the Court, although not quite finished. It is a very good looking building similar in appearance and plan to ours here." April 16, 1859. "Titus county. We were at Mt Pleasant court last week. The old court house was sold during the first week and the new brick Court House will be up before the next term." May 7, 1859 "Bonham has improved. The new courthouse going up in the center of town has risen one story. It is large enough to look well, 60 feet square and is a substantial work. The brick the Mortar the heavy bois d'arc timbers inside above the windows and doors, the handsome stone faced fireplaces and the frames of the openings are all good and give promise to the *best* courthouse in North Texas." December 17, 1859

47. July 10, 1847

48. He later was an unsuccessful candidate for Governor in 1849. Mills County was named in his honor. The Texas State Historical Association, *The Handbook of Texas* (Vol. II) at p. 200; see also *Handbook of Texas Online*, at http://www.tsha.utexas.edu/handbook/online/articles/MM/fmi38.htm

49. September 28, 1843

50. April 6, 1843

51. December 3, 1859

52. September 3, 1842

53. The Texas State Historical Association, *The Handbook of Texas* (Vol. II) at pp. 784 - 785; see also *Handbook of Texas Online*, at http://www.tsha.utexas.edu/handbook/online/articles/TT/fto8.html

54. March 19, 1859

55. April 2, 1859

56. April 14, 1860

57. April 14, 1860

58. Young Todd, also educated in Virginia, became a lawyer in Texas in 1860 and, a year later enlisted to fight for the Confederacy. Reaching the rank of captain, he was wounded at Antietam. After the war, he returned to the practice of law in Jefferson, became a District Attorney, until removed as "an impediment of reconstruction", the fate of many Texans who did not cooperate with the federal government during the Reconstruction. The Texas State Historical Association, *The Handbook of Texas* (Vol. II) at pp. 784 - 785

59. April 28, 1860

60. In 1803, when the United States had purchased the Louisiana Territory from the French, it claimed that part of the purchase included a part of eastern Texas - an ill-defined strip of land, running from Arroyo Hondo on the east and the Sabine River on the west. Called the Neutral Ground, both countries barred anyone from settling there and left it as a buffer between them.

61. The strip was to be ceded, by treaty, to the United States in 1821, but the policy of maintaining a buffer between the Texas territory and the United States persisted and resulted in the creation of a zone, 20 leagues - some 60 miles - wide from the U.S. border, in which Texas settlers were not permitted to reside under pain of losing the privileges granted them by Mexico. The number of settlers that ignored the Mexican prohibition was not insignificant. In fact, it has been estimated that, at the start of the Texas Revolution, fully half of the entire Texas population lived in this forbidden zone. After independence from Mexico was secured, this buffer zone became Harrison, Shelby and Panola counties. Apparently, some of the residents of these counties, had grown accustomed to living without the presence of the law in their communities. They did not take easily to the change, especially the Court system and its delays. When Dr. John Hansford was appointed District Judge, the situation worsened, and factions developed among the citizenry

62. April 24, 1844

63. August. 28, 1844

64. August 28, 1844

65. *Harrison County - We hear from Marshall that the District Court for Harrison County is still in session and probably will be for some days to come. Those persons who had committed offenses*

against the criminal law of the country, have, most of them, surrendered themselves for trial, and everything, we are told, commences in as orderly manner as in any community.

The Collector of customs . . . is receiving reports of importations and will proceed to collect the duties which, we are told, the citizens are resolved to pay.

We are glad to hear all of this. We welcome the return of those people to the performance of their duty to their fellow citizens and the Government, and we are very sure that, if their present course is persisted in, will work to their own pecuniary benefit, as well as to elevate their reputation as an honest and law abiding population. October 30, 1844

66. November 20, 1844

67. The Texas State Historical Association, *The Handbook of Texas* (Vol. II) at pp. 443 -444I; see also *Handbook of Texas Online*, at http://www.tsha.utexas.edu/handbook/online/articles/RR/fre2.html

After his days at a Judge he was elected United States congressman from the Eastern District of Texas. On January 15, 1861, Reagan resigned his congressional seat. Two weeks later he returned to Texas; for the next four years he served the Confederate States of America And later became Confederate postmaster general, captured imprisoned, he later was re elected.

68. May 21, 1853

69. May 31, 1856

70. The Texas State Historical Association, *The Handbook of Texas (Vol. I)* at p. 426; see also *Handbook of Texas Online,* at http://www.tsha.utexas.edu/handbook/online/articles/BB/fbu27.html

71. He thanked Judge John Reagan for sending DeMorse "currant grape vines that arrived in growable condition." February19, 1859. He also thanked Judge Ochiltree who "furnished us with several green heads of Prussian rye from the plantation of William A. Lawrence at Mound Prairie in Anderson county." July 1, 1848

72. November 1, 1856

73. November 29, 1856

74. *Handbook of Texas Online*, http://www.tsha.utexas.edu/handbook/online/articles/MM/fmaec.htm l

75. April 7, 1844

76. September 9, 1848

77. September 18, 1852

78. December 19,1857

79. The Texas State Historical Association, *The Handbook of Texas* (Vol. I) at p.527; see also *Handbook of Texas Online* at http://www.tsha.utexas.edu/handbook/online/articles/EE/fev12.html

80. April 23, 1853

81. May 14, 1853

82. May 14, 1853

83. April 9, 1859

84. December 3, 1859

85. *Handbook of Texas Online*, http://www.tsha.utexas.edu/handbook/online/articles/MM/fmaec.htm l

86. September 3, 1859

87. Edward H. Tarrant was born in South Carolina in 1799 and lived in Kentucky, then Tennessee. He gravitated toward soldiering. He was elected a colonel of militia. In 1830, he moved to Red River county, Texas and seven years later and was elected to represent the county in the House of Representatives of the Second Congress. He resigned that position as too tame and opted to direct Ranger activities against the Indians. It came easy to him and by 1839 was elected brigadier general in command of an organization of Northeast Texas defenders known as the Fourth Brigade. He is most remembered for his victory Village Creek, an almost sacred spot DeMorse would visit in his roaming about. Later he lived at Chambers Creek in Ellis County, where DeMorse frequently visited when he was down that way. In 1857, when Indians were making trouble again in that area, he again turned his energy to fighting them. The Texas State Historical Association, *The Handbook of Texas* at p. 707.

88. There were a few exceptions. The Red River county firm of Sutton & Sutton had it main office in Clarksville but a branch one in the country in Kiamitia, for R. Peterson, Attorney at Law

89. February 5, 1859

90. April 23,1859

91. February 12, 1859

92. February 26, 1859

93. It was the "mob" that was seeking the extinction of lawyers not ordinary yeoman/citizens. The mob was lawless. We would be remiss, however, in not noting that the English mob would evolve into American colonists who did throw out one law and bring in another.

94. June 30, 1860

95. May 21, 1853

96. May 21, 1853

97. April 20, 1850

98. July 21, 1849

99. December 19,1857

100. *E.g.* "Notice by John B. Carter that he has lost or mislaid his Head Right certificates, and those of James Berry, Wm. Y. Lacey and William McCown and that, if not found, he will apply for new ones." August 20, 1842. The history of land grants in Texas goes back to Spanish and Mexican times. Its purpose was to encourage colonization of the vast vacant region. In 1836 the first Congress of the Republic of Texas continued the practice as did the State of Texas when it joined the United States, officially recognizing the land grants made under Spanish and Mexican rule as valid. Head right grants were given by the Republic on the condition that specified requirements be met by the grantees. Under the Constitution of 1836 all heads of white families living in Texas on March 4, 1836,were granted"first class" head rights of one league and one labor (4,605.5 acres), and single men aged seventeen years or older, one-third of a league (1,476.1 acres). Later, there were "second class", "third class" and "fourth class" head rights of differing sizes depending on when they arrived in Texas and how long they stayed. A total of 36,876,492 acres was granted by the Republic in head right certificates.

Both the Republic and state granted lands for military service in the form of bounty and donation grants.

101. November 5, 1859

102. May 12, 1860

103. August 2, 1842

104. "Berkley J. Fuller will apply on the first Saturday in May next, for a discharge in Bankruptcy before the Chief Judge of Fannin County." April 13, 1843

105. August 20, 1842

106. *Charles DeMorse, Pioneer Editor and Statesman*, by Ernest Wallace, at p. 13.

107. As reported in Pat B. Clark's *The History of Clarksville and Old Red River County, Texas*

108. The term "posse" - men summoned by a peace officer to assist him in making an arrest - has an undeniable western ring to it. Actually, its roots are much older and originated in Britain. The Latin *posse comitatus* means literally "the power or force of the county," that is, its citizens protecting the common good.

109. Some thirty years after, Jim Clark, a Clarksville lawyer and kin to the town's founder, appeared in court in Mississippi. He was approached by an affluent, upstanding townsman who inquired whether Dr. George Gordon of Clarksville was still alive. When advised that he was, the stranger revealed himself as the spared felon and asked Clark to pass along the message that he was the man Dr. Gordon and the gracious women of Clarksville had saved that day and that he would be forever grateful for the life that had been restored him.

110. Con artists are not recent creations as evidenced by the following item:

> *Two men named Flynt and Mullens were arrested in Town on the first day of Court last week, upon suspicion of Negro stealing and dealing in counterfeit coins. The two men are residents of Harrison County and on their way home from Arkansas, having a Negro man with them as they passed through here. The circumstances connected with the transaction are of a most suspicious character. The Negro had made an appointment with a Negro of Mr. William Donoho, to meet him the night of the day they had left town. Mr. Donoho's Negro suspected and, at night, at the appointed time, the Negro of Mullens came for him and was arrested and confined; and, on being searched, was found in*

possession of $320 of counterfeit American gold.

The Negro stated several things against the men Flynt and Mullens, and among others, said that he had been sold several times (giving the names of the purchasers) and then run off again by Flynt.

In the morning, Mullens came in looking for his Negro and was arrested. At night, a party of citizens pursued Flynt, who was found on the other side of the Sulphur. Mullens and Flynt are under a bond to appear at the next term of the District Court. The Negro has escaped. October 16, 1844

111. Coins were usually not counterfeited and paper money was not yet in circulation in the United States. Rather, bank notes, issued on out of state banks – Texas law did not allow banks at the time – were usually the instruments altered.

COUNTERFEITERS

Counterfeiters have been in operation in St. Francisville. Spurious notes of the Louisiana State Bank and the State Bank of Indiana were set afoot. An individual who passed some of the money was pursued as far as Waterloo where he was arrested and brought back. March 16, 1843

112. *Smuggling - We understand that goods to a large amount have recently been smuggled into the Country near the mouth of the Sabine River. This has been effected by clearing small vessels to New Orleans for some point in the southwest corner of Louisiana, which instead of stopping at their ostensible destination, proceeded to uninhabited spots on our own coast between the mouths of the Sabine and Trinity Rivers and there discharged their cargoes which, from there, were hauled into the interior.* June 22, 1843

113. DeMorse was quick to warn the community of risks like this. For example:

FRAUDULENT LAND TITLES

We would advise our friends, and the public to be on their guard in respect, to the Land titles of De Leon's colony, as we learn from a respectable gentleman of Western Texas, that the late commissioner of that colony, who has been residing in Mexico since the revolution, has lately returned to Victoria, and has brought with him many titles to Lands granted to members of his family, the originals of which are not and never have been filed in the General Land Office of the Republic of Texas, as by law required. Some of them are now offered for sale, and we understand that a number of titles have found their way to New Orleans for Market, where every exertion will be made to dispose of them to the innocent purchaser. June 21, 1845

However, it is likely that, if a law were broken here, it was the claimant under the Spanish land grant that was being treated illegally, not the Texans who now claimed title to those lands. Before the Revolution, the Colony of DeLeon was comprised almost entirely of Mexican colonists, although some Irish and Italian settlers had also been recruited to the Colony. All the townspeople, including the Mexican settlers fought on behalf of the Republic of Texas against Mexico. But, after the Battle of Goliad, white Texans attacked the Mexican population of DeLeon and attempted to drive them from their land, with some success. The titles in dispute here may well have been those of the Mexicans driven off their land.

114. September 17, 1859

115. February 19, 1959

116. October 8, 1859

117. January 8, 1859

118. December 3, 1859

119. December 24, 1859

120. *"Mr. Alt Davis, sheriff of Fannin county, passed through town this morning, having in charge the man named Rozell who killed Castleberry in Lamar county last year. Rozell broke jail in Bonham sometime ago and was arrested again in Gainesville. We understand that he assisted in the stampede from the Cooke jail a few days ago. He is certainly an ingenious fellow but his talent wouldn't save him this time as he will be heavily ironed when in the Bonham jail."* October 8, 1859

121. September 24, 1859

122. *"Our agent in Weatherford, Parker county, writes to us dated April 30, that the district court for Palo Pinto county (the first) was held the previous week and that a Spyres was sentenced to the penitentiary for hog stealing. As it is customary in the penitentiary to put a man back to work at his old calling, if he has any, our*

correspondent wants to know how the state will avail itself of this man's skill at his old business. May 14, 1859

123. May 25, 1843

124. October 8, 1859

125. An interesting glimpse of the both operations of a gang of horse thieves and the criminal justice system, which exchanged a light sentence with one defendant for a list of the other gang members.

> *The large number of horses stolen from our citizens in Texas has become the most alarming evil and led in some cases to the summary vengeance of the Lynch law.*
>
> *We lay before our readers a confession of a horse thief at a late term of the Court of Burleson County. We trust that it may lead to the breaking up of the horse thievery gang declared to be in existence in this state and well organized.*
>
> *"When he [Hugh Allen] first came to Texas, he met with Tom Middleton at Buck Horn in Austin. The accused was drunk at that place. Tom Middleton employed him to work for him. They immediately left Buck Horn for the town of Bastrop and, at the direction of Middleton, the accused stole a horse; then they started for the town of LaGrange and, on their way, stole two horses, one a paint . Middleton, up until this point, never told the accused that he was engaged in the regular employment of horse stealing. They then stole two on the Colorado River and, then on their way back to the town of Chappell Hill, Washington County, they stole three, a little black, a bay, a sorrel. They then stole two, a bay and a brown at the White's, near Colonel Kirby's. Accused said that they often stole horses in the day as well as in the night. They then went to Col. Wm. Sledge's plantation, where they stole an old black mule. Middleton then went up the country to Mr. Griffiths for the purposes of stealing a fine horse. He did not succeed, but stole two others on his return. The accused stated that he had been engaged in stealing*

horses with the following named persons, to wit: Nat Berry, Bill Berry, both killed at San Antonio; three of the Samuels, who live down the county; three Batton boys, who live on Lost Creek, Hillard Putnam and Vandy Putnam; he does not know where they live as they are young men having no wives; old Jim Cox, Burleson county, William Hutton, Reuben Dean, Washington County; Thomas Taylor of Eastern Texas, John Ake, a large raw boned man with sandy hair who lives in Arkansas and visits Texas for the purpose of stealing horses.

The accused says he has been shot at since he was in jail and thinks that Middleton did it, as he sent word that he intended to kill him for telling on the party. The accused was raised in the state of Alabama and came to Texas in July 1856. The name of his mother is Little; he is an illegitimate. The name of the man who raised him is Joe Allen and lives in Benton county, Alabama.

Accused stated that Tom Middleton had informed him that he [Middldton] had killed a Jew pedlar and took from him all his valuable property; this occurred in one of the lower counties.

The Jury then received the charge of the Judge and retired to consider verdict. They returned in ten minutes with the verdict of guilty, assessing the penalty as two years at hard labor in the penitentiary.
December 12, 1857

126. November 7, 1857

127. November 7, 1857

128. June 19, 1858

129. *F.G. Barnhart, confined within the County Jail [Red River] for horse theft for the last week, was on Wednesday last brought before DK Jamison, Esq and ,after a thorough examination, bound over in the sum of $800 to appear at the next term of the District Court.*
November 5, 1859

130. August 17, 1861

131. October 19, 1861

132. January 1, 1859

133. April 16, 1859

134. November 12, 1859

135. November 12, 1859

136. January 18, 1859

137. June 25, 1859

138. January 8, 1859

139. June 25, 1859

140. January 8, 1859

141. January 29, 1859

142. March 3, 1858

143. July 31, 1844

144. July 31, 1844 . "Two [other] men, Ireland and Harris, were arrested but convicted of nothing more than theft, were made to hang the others."

145. July 31, 1844

146. October 29, 1853

147. June 25, 1859

148. January 15, 1859

149. December 19, 1857

150. June 28, 1858

151. November 27, 1852

152. April 23, 1853

153. April 23, 1853

154. Reuben A. Reeves was from Kentucky and practiced law in Anderson County., Texas. In 1857, Reeves was elected district judge in Palestine. In August 1864, during the Confederacy he was elected Associate Justice of the Texas Supreme Court. After the War, he was elected district court judge but was removed from office on November 30, 1867, as an "obstruction to Reconstruction." Later, he

was reappointed Associate Justice of the Supreme Court. *Handbook of Texas Online*,.http://www.tsha.utexas.edu/handbook/online/articles/RR/fre23.html

155. May 14, 1853

156. April 2, 1853

157. March 18, 1854

158. November 28, 1857

159. Know Nothingism, cloaked in secrecy, was an anti-immigrant and anti Catholic sentiment. There had been considerable unhappiness among the native born citizens of English /Scotch Irish/Dutch descent with the influx of Irish and other Catholic foreigners. DeMorse was not among them. While no one could accuse him of being fond of "Popery", he detested their persecutors. *The Standard* reprinted accounts from its eastern exchanges of the mob conduct of the party's members - church burnings in Boston, Massachusetts and in Bath, Maine; a Catholic priest tarred and feathered at Ellsworth, Maine pursuant to a vote taken at town meeting; riots in Newark, Philadelphia, and St Louis, among them. Soon the mob moved from the street to the polls.

DeMorse was fond of his "dimes" as he called the money he earned from selling his papers. But he even bragged about not caring about losing them because he alienated Know Nothing readers.

> *The "15 Know Nothings" [from Grayson] addressed a letter to the editor of this newspaper and who, in conclusion, very politely said to us: "You will do us the favor not to send your newspaper to us any longer. You will please send your accounts to your agent here (if you have any here) and we will [pay him] what we respectively owe you" had very much raised our hopes of making a tolerable collection in Grayson but [did not]. Whether in politics or payments, we fear their characters are very unreliable. They are gay deceivers.* November 17, 1855.

160. September 29, 1860

161. December 17, 1859

162. December 17, 1859

163. December 31, 1859

164. December 12, 1846
165. May 12, 1855
166. June 4, 1853
167. May 8, 1858
168. March 23, 1850
169. March 23, 1850
170. May 12, 1855
171. May 28, 1853
172. May 14, 1853
173. February 16, 1850
174. November 17, 1859
175. June 12, 1858
176. May 8, 1858
177. May 28, 1859
178. May 8, 1858
179. June 4, 1853
180. June , 19, 1859
181. July 3, 1852
182. July 17, 1852
183. June 4, 1853
184. August 27, 1859
185. January 1, 1859
186. January 1, 1859
187. April 16, 1853
188. April 16, 1853
189. April 16, 1853
190. April 16, 1853
191. July 3, 1852
192. May 5, 1855
193. May 5, 1855

194. May 5, 1855

195. May 5, 1855

196. April 16, 1859

197. April 9, 1853

198. The next week, in Hunt County, an offer to match the mortified Uncle Andy with a three year old steer, made by the owner of the Greenville Inn, "came in too late for acceptance, Uncle Andy leaving this morning for the Supreme Court." April 16, 1853

199. For the remainder of the day's races "Choctaw, after winning one heat, was beaten by Frosty. Frosty, in turn, was bested by the Dumpling Sorrel and, last of all, came a pretty and well contested race between Bolivar and Cass, in which Bolivar beat the General by a little." April 9, 1853

200. April 9,1853

201. April 9, 1853

202. May 5, 1855

203. May 14, 1853

204. May 21, 1853

205. April 17, 1858

206. April 17, 1858

207. May 28, 1853

208. May 14, 1853

209. Demorse reported an antelope at Fort Worth, which, "had been for months one of the pets of the place but had died form eating a poisonous weed." In Parker county, DeMorse's party encountered "an antelope, which stood in the road before us and stood so long that we supposed him to be a pet. But, as the foremost riders approached him, he skipped away in a semi circle and so continued to do as if playing around us for some time until we lost sight of him in some valley close by." June 19th, 1858

210 June 12, 1858

211. May 14, 1853

212. May 14, 1853

213. April 23, 1853
214. May 14, 1853
215. July 3, 1858
216. January 1, 1859
217. January 1, 1859
218. August 7, 1852
219. July 3, 1858
220. June 26, 1858
221. June 12, 1858
222. June 19, 1858
223. May 14, 1853
224. June 12, 1858
225. June 19, 1858
226. May 5, 1855
227. June 19, 1857
228. July 24, 1851
229. July 31, 1852
230. May 14, 1853
231. May 28, 1853
232. July 3, 1858
233. February 2, 1850
234. July 19, 1852
235. June 4, 1853
236. May 28, 1853
237. May 28, 1853
238. June 18, 1859
239. June 23, 1860
240. December 22, 1960
241. Latin for "it doesn't exist."

242 January 26, 1861

243. February 9, 1861

244. February 23, 1861

245. March 2, 1861

246. March 23, 186

247. October 19, 1861

248. May 11, 1861

249. October 19, 1861

250. December 21, 1861

251. August 17, 1861

252. May 11, 1861

253. He had been the roommate of Stonewall Jackson at West Point. *Handbook of Texas Online*, http://www.tsha.utexas.edu/handbook/online/articles/MM/fma85.htm l

254. After the war, Maxey was elected to the United States Senate on January 28, 1874 and served two terms. http://www.tsha.utexas.edu/handbook/online/articles/MM/fma85.htm l

255. Upon his return to Texas after the war, he was elected judge of the Sixteenth Judicial District, Dallas, but was removed by Gen. Philip Sheridan as "impediment to Reconstruction." *Handbook of Texas Online*, http://www.tsha.utexas.edu/handbook/online/articles/GG/fgo8.html

256. In 1864 Burford offered his resignation, admitting that he did not possess the ability to lead troops in combat. His commanding officers agreed, commended his patriotism, and accepted the resignation. After the war, he resumed sitting on the bench but was removed by Gen. Philip H. Sheridan as an"impediment to Reconstruction." The Texas State Historical Association, *The Handbook of Texas (Vol. I)* at p. 426; see also *Handbook of Texas Online,* at http://www.tsha.utexas.edu/handbook/online/articles/BB/fbu27.html

257. *Handbook of Texas Online*, http://www.tsha.utexas.edu/handbook/online/articles/WW/qkw3.html

258. May 4, 1861

259. December 21, 1861

260. *Handbook of Texas Online*, s.v. http://www.tsha.utexas.edu/handbook/online/articles/OO/foc2.html .

261. May11, 1861
262. October 19, 1861
263. July 20, 1861
264. July 20, 1861
265. July 27, 1861
266. May11, 1861
267. May11, 1861
268. November 23, 1861
269. November 23, 1861
270. *Handbook of Texas Online*, s.v.
http://www.tsha.utexas.edu/handbook/online/articles/BB/fbapw.html
271. May 25, 1861
272. May 25, 1861
273. *Handbook of Texas Online*, s.v.
http://www.tsha.utexas.edu/handbook/online/articles/EE/fep1.html
274. *Handbook of Texas Online*,
http://www.tsha.utexas.edu/handbook/online/articles/HH/fhace.html
275. *Handbook of Texas Online*,
http://www.tsha.utexas.edu/handbook/online/articles/HH/fhace.html
276. October 5, 1861
277. May 11, 1861
278. *Handbook of Texas Online*,
.http://www.tsha.utexas.edu/handbook/online/articles/BB/fbu36.hml

INDICES

PEOPLE

Places in Texas

Places Outside of Texas

General Index

Printed in Dunstable, United Kingdom

91218265R00097